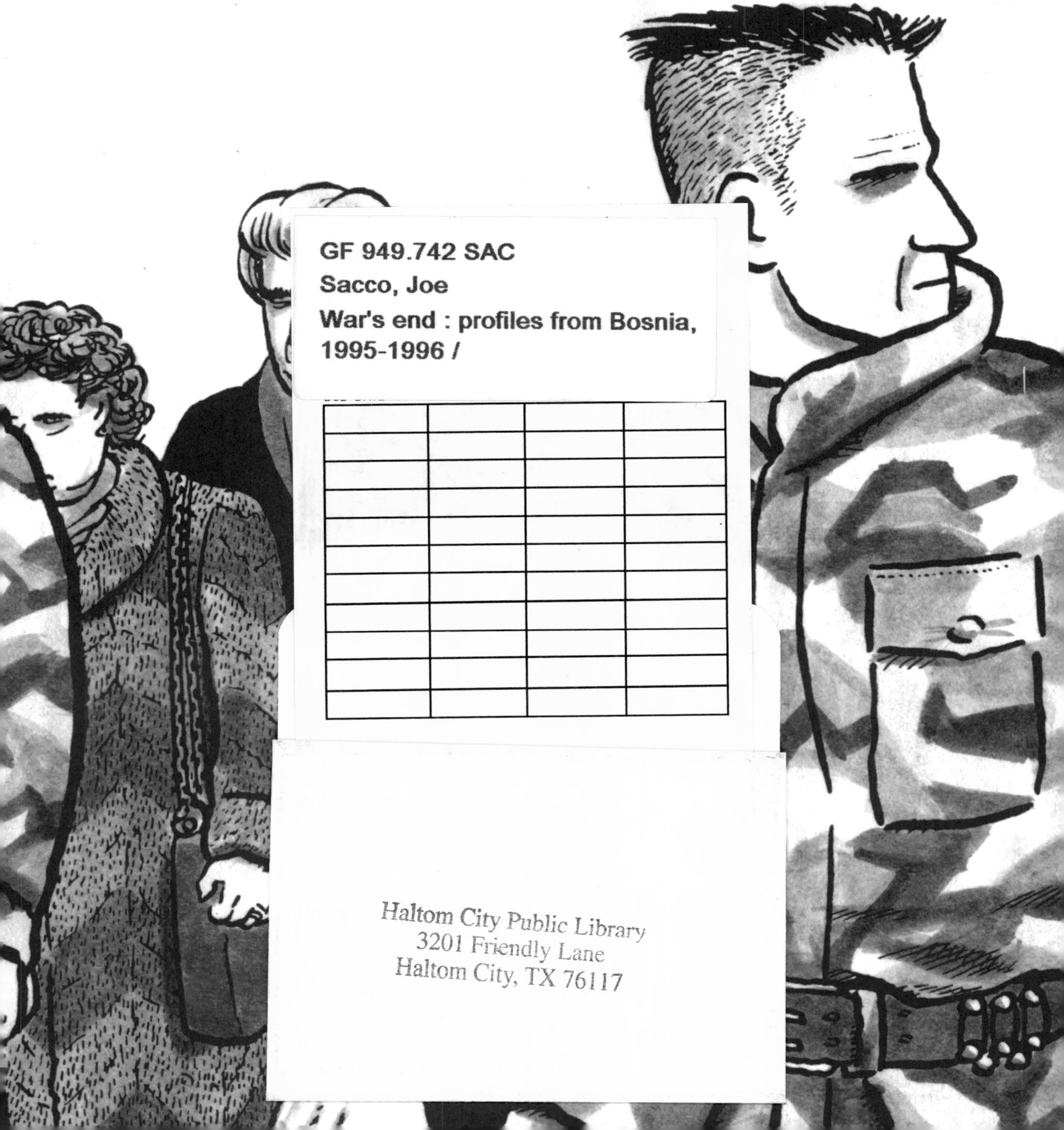

JOE SACCO

WAR'S END

PROFILES FROM BOSNIA 1995-96

Publication design: Michel Vrána, Black Eye Design.
Publisher: Chris Oliveros.
Publicity: Peggy Burns.

"Christmas With Karadzic" originally appeared in ZERO ZERO #15, published by Fantagraphics Books. "Soba" originally appeared in STORIES FROM BOSNIA #1, published by Drawn & Quarterly.

DRAWN & QUARTERLY
Post Office Box 48056
Montreal, Quebec
Canada H2V 4S8
www.drawnandquarterly.com

First hardcover edition: June 2005.
Printed in Singapore.
10 9 8 7 6 5 4 3 2 1

Library and Archives Canada Cataloguing in Publication

Sacco, Joe
War's End : Profiles from Bosnia, 1995-96 / Joe Sacco.

ISBN 1-896597-92-0

1. Seric-Shoba, Nebojsa--Comic books, strips, etc.
2. Karadzic, Radovan V., 1945- --Comic books, strips, etc.
3. Yugoslav War, 1991-1995--Comic books, strips, etc.
4. Bosnia and Hercegovina--History--1992- --Comic books,
strips, etc. I. Title.

DR1313.3.S23 2005   949.74203   C2004-906909-8

Distributed in the USA by:
FARRAR, STRAUS AND GIROUX
19 Union Square West
New York, NY 10003
Orders: 888.330.8477

Distributed in Canada by:
RAINCOAST BOOKS
9050 Shaughnessy Street
Vancouver, BC V6P 6E5
Orders: 800.663.5714

JOE SACCO

WAR'S END

PROFILES FROM BOSNIA 1995-96

DRAWN AND QUARTERLY BOOKS

ALSO BY JOE SACCO:

THE FIXER
Drawn & Quarterly

NOTES FROM A DEFEATIST
Fantagraphics Books

SAFE AREA GORAZDE: THE WAR IN EASTERN BOSNIA 1992-95
Fantagraphics Books

PALESTINE
Fantagraphics Books

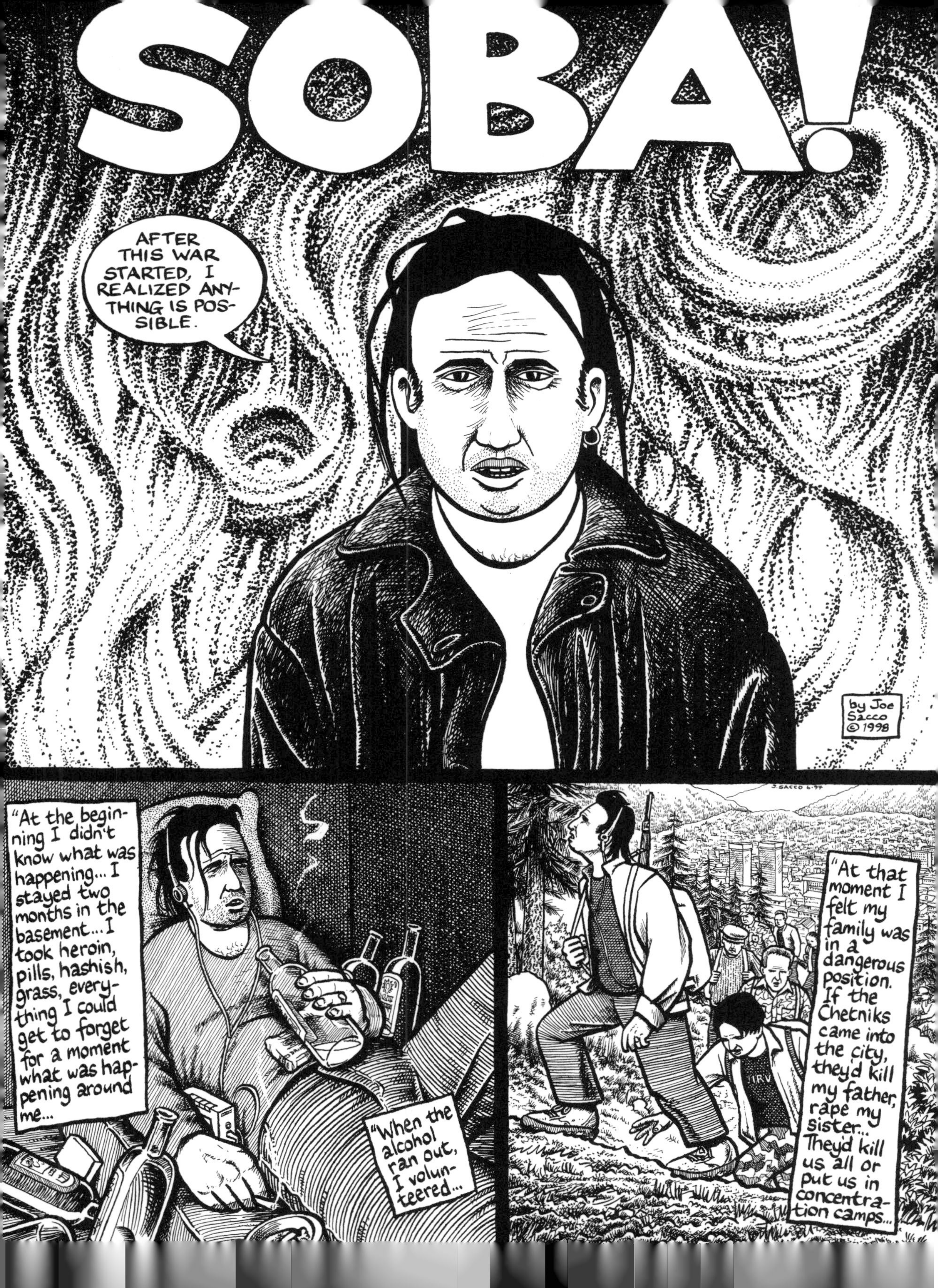
SOBA!
AFTER THIS WAR STARTED, I REALIZED ANYTHING IS POSSIBLE.
by Joe Sacco © 1998
"At the beginning I didn't know what was happening... I stayed two months in the basement... I took heroin, pills, hashish, grass, everything I could get to forget for a moment what was happening around me...
"When the alcohol ran out, I volunteered...
"At that moment I felt my family was in a dangerous position. If the Chetniks came into the city, they'd kill my father, rape my sister... They'd kill us all or put us in concentration camps...

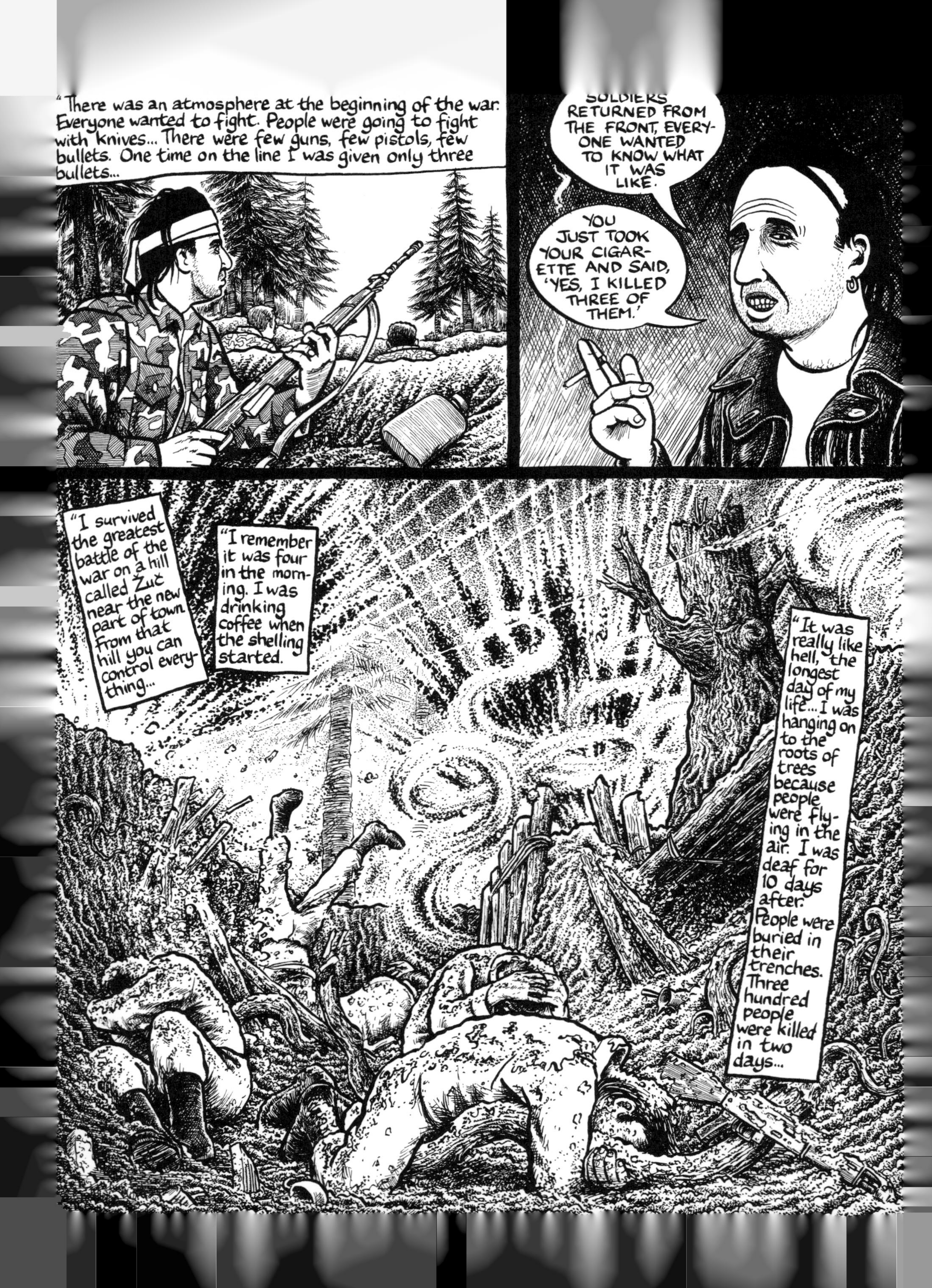
"There was an atmosphere at the beginning of the war. Everyone wanted to fight. People were going to fight with knives... There were few guns, few pistols, few bullets. One time on the line I was given only three bullets...
SOLDIERS RETURNED FROM THE FRONT, EVERYONE WANTED TO KNOW WHAT IT WAS LIKE.
YOU JUST TOOK YOUR CIGARETTE AND SAID, 'YES, I KILLED THREE OF THEM.'
J. SACCO 6.97
"I survived the greatest battle of the war on a hill called Žuč near the new part of town. From that hill you can control everything...
"I remember it was four in the morning. I was drinking coffee when the shelling started.
"It was really like hell, the longest day of my life... I was hanging on to the roots of trees because people were flying in the air. I was deaf for 10 days after. People were buried in their trenches. Three hundred people were killed in two days...

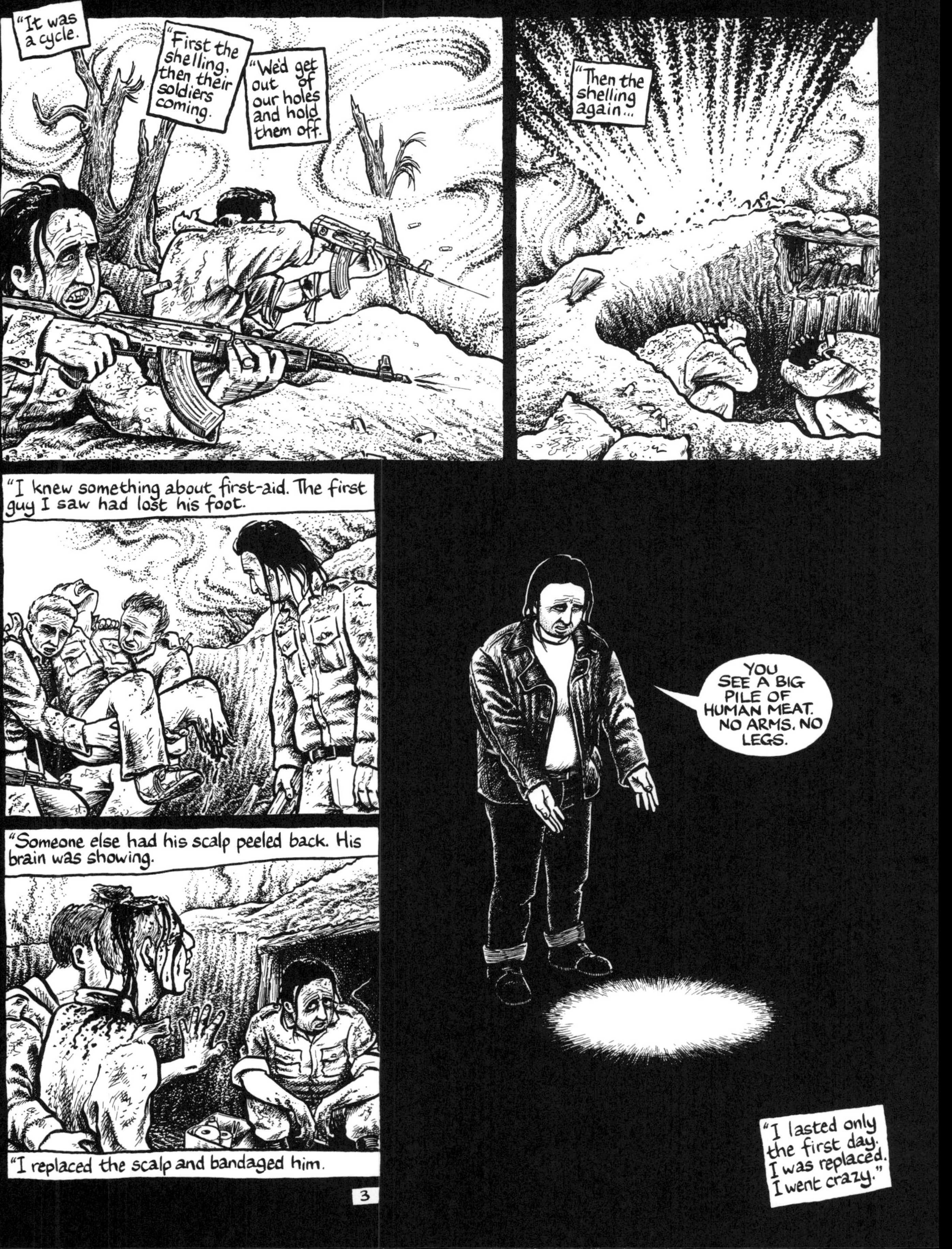
"It was a cycle.
"First the shelling, then their soldiers coming.
"We'd get out of our holes and hold them off.
"Then the shelling again...
"I knew something about first-aid. The first guy I saw had lost his foot.
"Someone else had his scalp peeled back. His brain was showing.
"I replaced the scalp and bandaged him.
YOU SEE A BIG PILE OF HUMAN MEAT. NO ARMS, NO LEGS.
"I lasted only the first day. I was replaced. I went crazy."

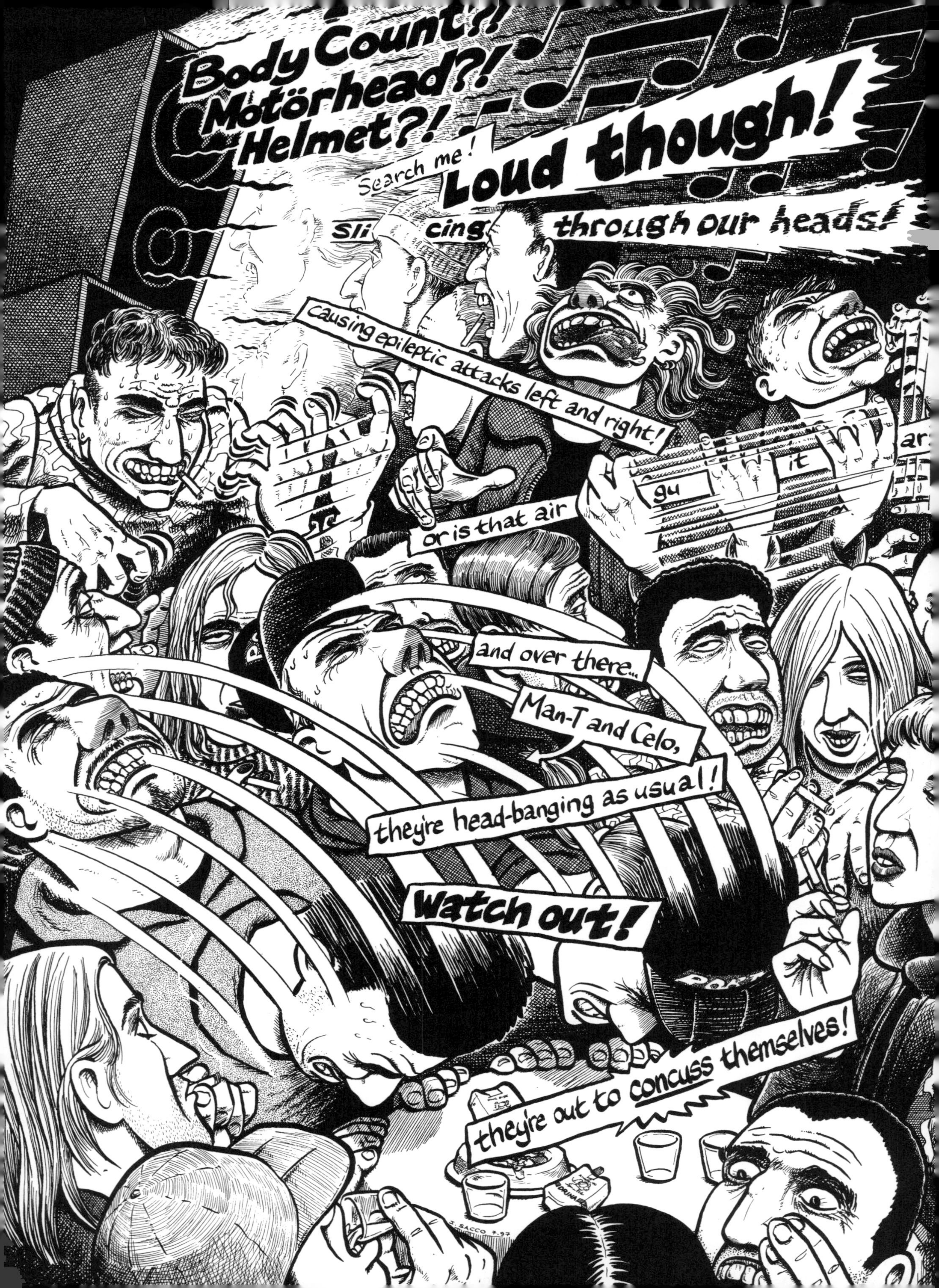
Body Count?! Motörhead?! Helmet?!
Search me!
Loud though!
Sli cing through our heads!
causing epileptic attacks left and right!
or is that air gu it ar
and over there...
Man-T and Celo,
they're head-banging as usual!
Watch out!
they're out to concuss themselves!
J. SACCO

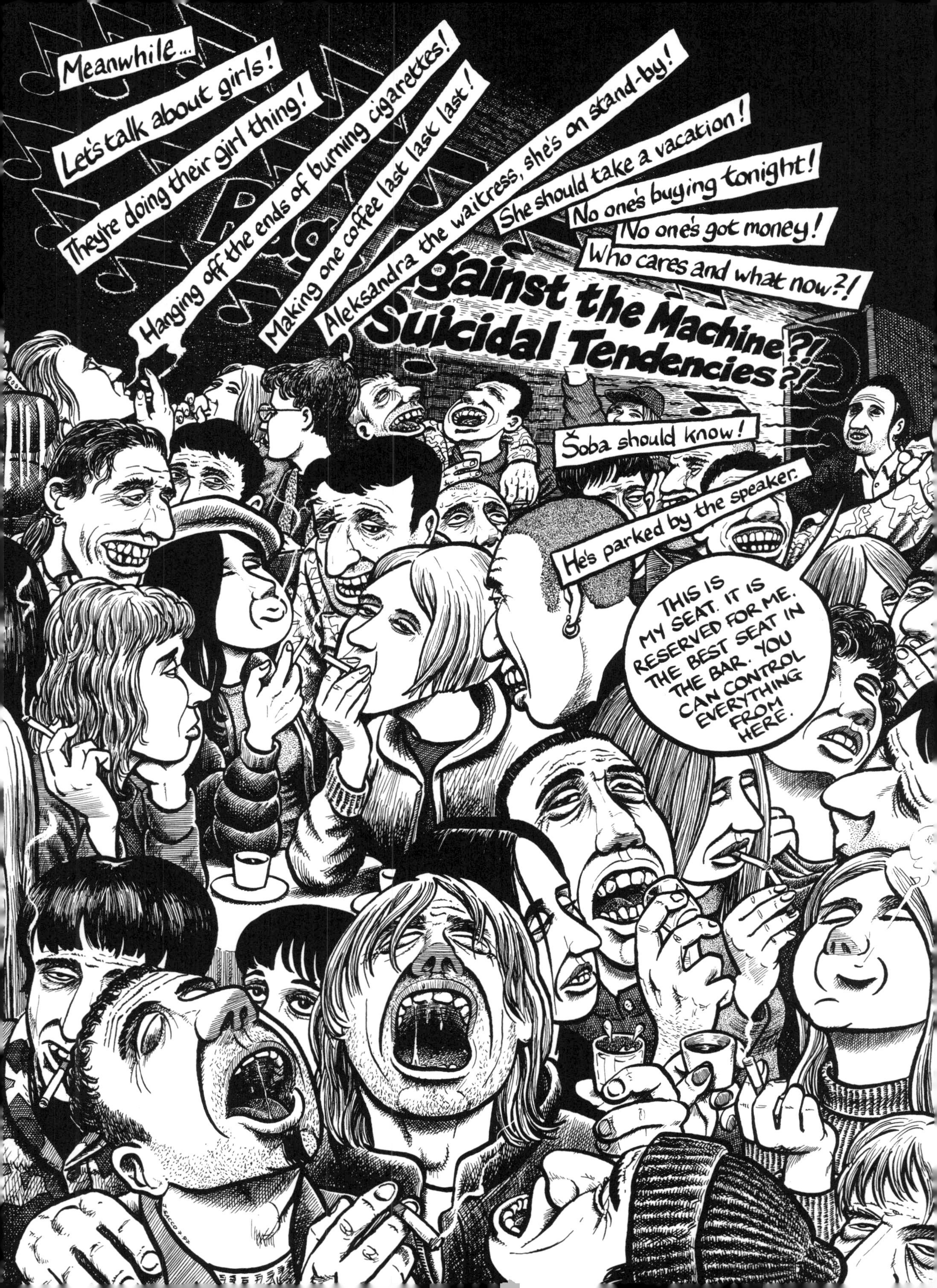

Meanwhile...
Let's talk about girls!
They're doing their girl thing!
Hanging off the ends of burning cigarettes!
Making one coffee last last last last!
Aleksandra the waitress, she's on stand-by!
She should take a vacation!
No one's buying tonight!
No one's got money!
Who cares and what now?!
Against the Machine?!
Suicidal Tendencies?!
Šoba should know!
He's parked by the speaker.
THIS IS MY SEAT. IT IS RESERVED FOR ME. THE BEST SEAT IN THE BAR. YOU CAN CONTROL EVERYTHING FROM HERE.

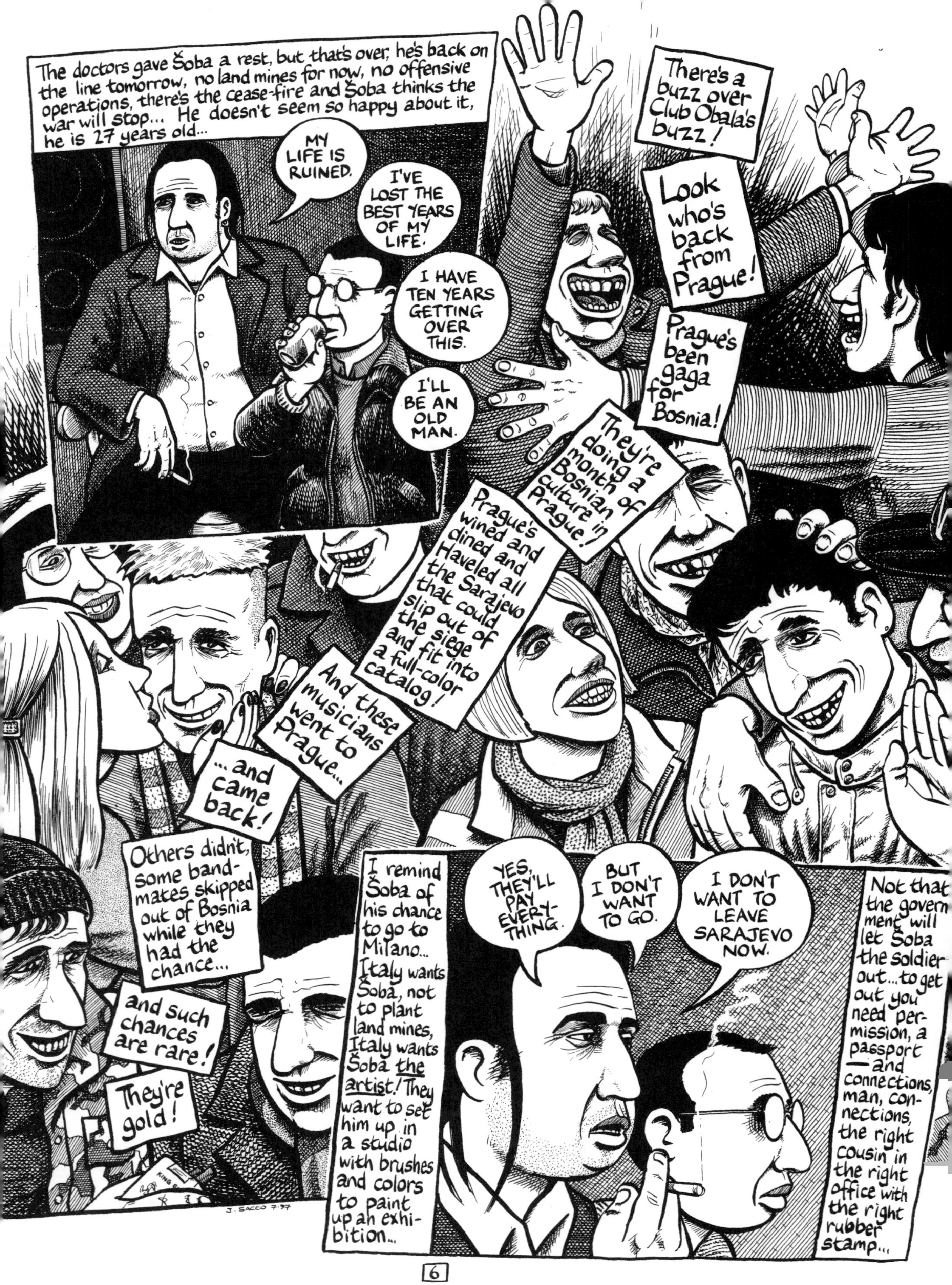
The doctors gave Šoba a rest, but that's over; he's back on the line tomorrow, no land mines for now, no offensive operations, there's the cease-fire and Šoba thinks the war will stop... He doesn't seem so happy about it, he is 27 years old...
MY LIFE IS RUINED.
I'VE LOST THE BEST YEARS OF MY LIFE.
I HAVE TEN YEARS GETTING OVER THIS.
I'LL BE AN OLD MAN.
There's a buzz over Club Obala's buzz!
Look who's back from Prague!
Prague's been gaga for Bosnia!
They're doing a month of Bosnian culture in Prague!
Prague's wined and dined and Haveled all the Sarajevo that could slip out of the siege and fit into a full-color catalog!
And these musicians went to Prague...
...and came back!
Others didn't, some band-mates skipped out of Bosnia while they had the chance...
and such chances are rare!
They're gold!
I remind Šoba of his chance to go to Milano... Italy wants Šoba, not to plant land mines, Italy wants Šoba the artist! They want to set him up in a studio with brushes and colors to paint up an exhibition...
YES, THEY'LL PAY EVERY-THING.
BUT I DON'T WANT TO GO.
I DON'T WANT TO LEAVE SARAJEVO NOW.
Not that the government will let Šoba the soldier out... to get out you need permission, a passport —and connections, man, connections, the right cousin in the right office with the right rubber stamp...
J. SACCO 7-97

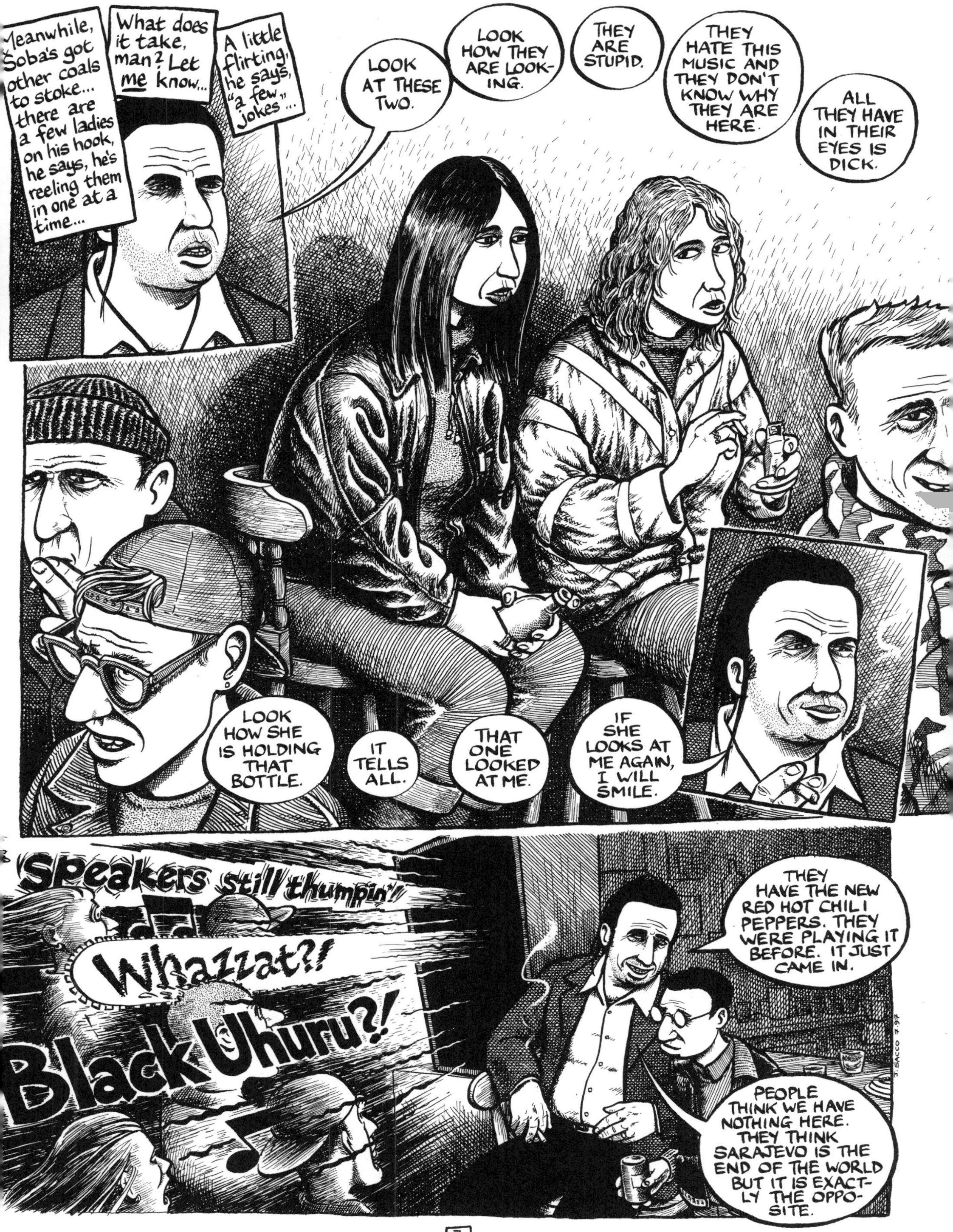
Meanwhile, Šoba's got other coals to stoke... there are a few ladies on his hook, he says, he's reeling them in one at a time...
What does it take, man? Let me know...
A little flirting, he says, "a few jokes"...
LOOK AT THESE TWO.
LOOK HOW THEY ARE LOOKING.
THEY ARE STUPID.
THEY HATE THIS MUSIC AND THEY DON'T KNOW WHY THEY ARE HERE.
ALL THEY HAVE IN THEIR EYES IS DICK.
LOOK HOW SHE IS HOLDING THAT BOTTLE.
IT TELLS ALL.
THAT ONE LOOKED AT ME.
IF SHE LOOKS AT ME AGAIN, I WILL SMILE.
Speakers still thumpin'!
Whazzat?!
Black Uhuru?!
THEY HAVE THE NEW RED HOT CHILI PEPPERS. THEY WERE PLAYING IT BEFORE. IT JUST CAME IN.
PEOPLE THINK WE HAVE NOTHING HERE. THEY THINK SARAJEVO IS THE END OF THE WORLD BUT IT IS EXACTLY THE OPPOSITE.
J. SACCO 7.97

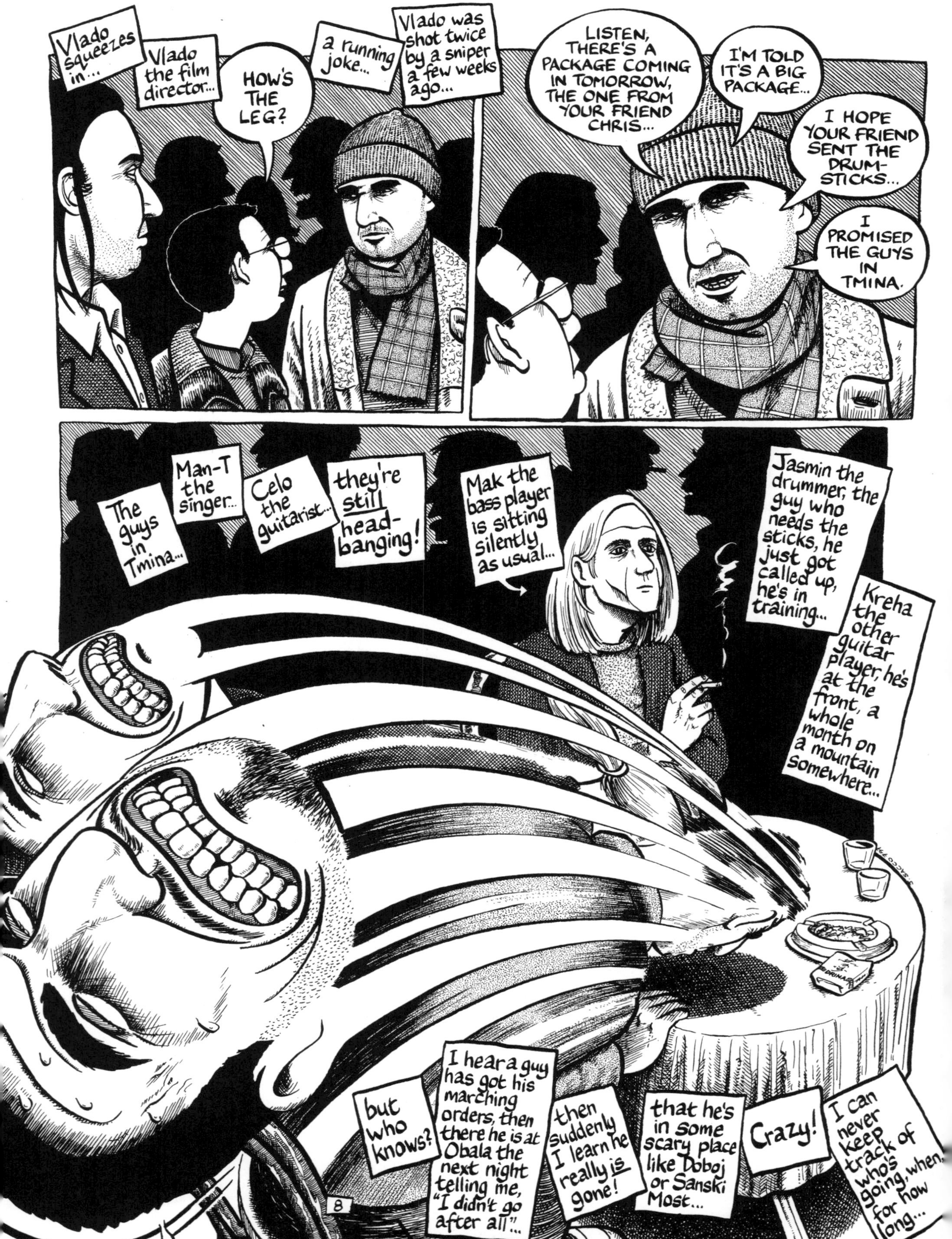

Vlado squeezes in...
Vlado the film director...
HOW'S THE LEG?
a running joke...
Vlado was shot twice by a sniper a few weeks ago...
LISTEN, THERE'S A PACKAGE COMING IN TOMORROW, THE ONE FROM YOUR FRIEND CHRIS...
I'M TOLD IT'S A BIG PACKAGE...
I HOPE YOUR FRIEND SENT THE DRUM-STICKS...
I PROMISED THE GUYS IN TMINA.
The guys in Tmina...
Man-T the singer...
Celo the guitarist...
they're still head-banging!
Mak the bass player is sitting silently as usual...
Jasmin the drummer, the guy who needs the sticks, he just got called up, he's in training...
Kreha the other guitar player, he's at the front, a whole month on a mountain somewhere...
but who knows?
I hear a guy has got his marching orders, then there he is at Obala the next night telling me, "I didn't go after all"...
then suddenly I learn he really is gone!
that he's in some scary place like Doboj or Sanski Most...
Crazy!
I can never keep track of who's going, when, for how long...

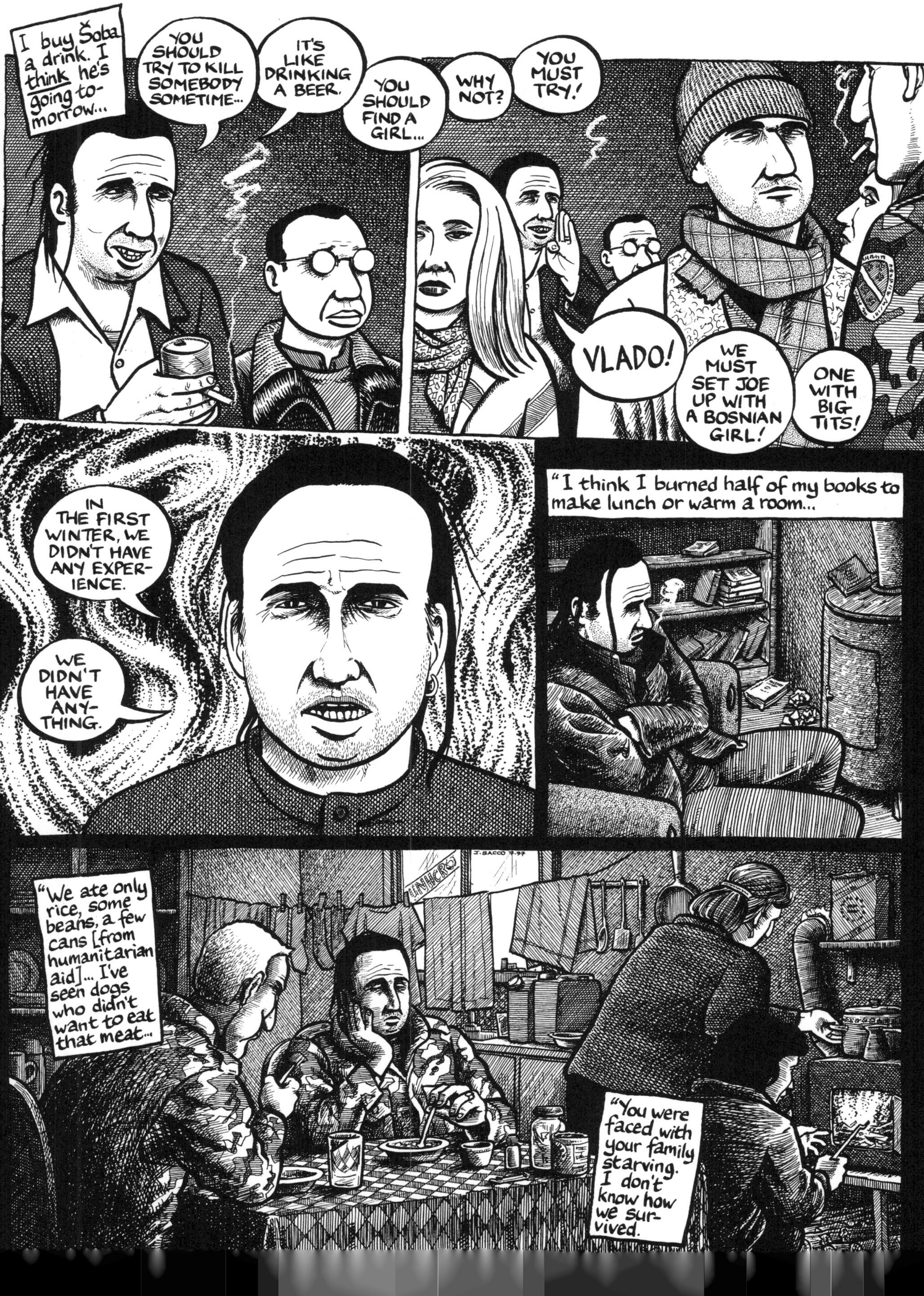
I buy Šoba a drink. I think he's going tomorrow...
YOU SHOULD TRY TO KILL SOMEBODY SOMETIME...
IT'S LIKE DRINKING A BEER.
YOU SHOULD FIND A GIRL...
WHY NOT?
YOU MUST TRY!
VLADO!
WE MUST SET JOE UP WITH A BOSNIAN GIRL!
ONE WITH BIG TITS!
IN THE FIRST WINTER, WE DIDN'T HAVE ANY EXPERIENCE.
WE DIDN'T HAVE ANYTHING.
"I think I burned half of my books to make lunch or warm a room...
J. SACCO
"We ate only rice, some beans, a few cans [from humanitarian aid]... I've seen dogs who didn't want to eat that meat...
"You were faced with your family starving. I don't know how we survived.

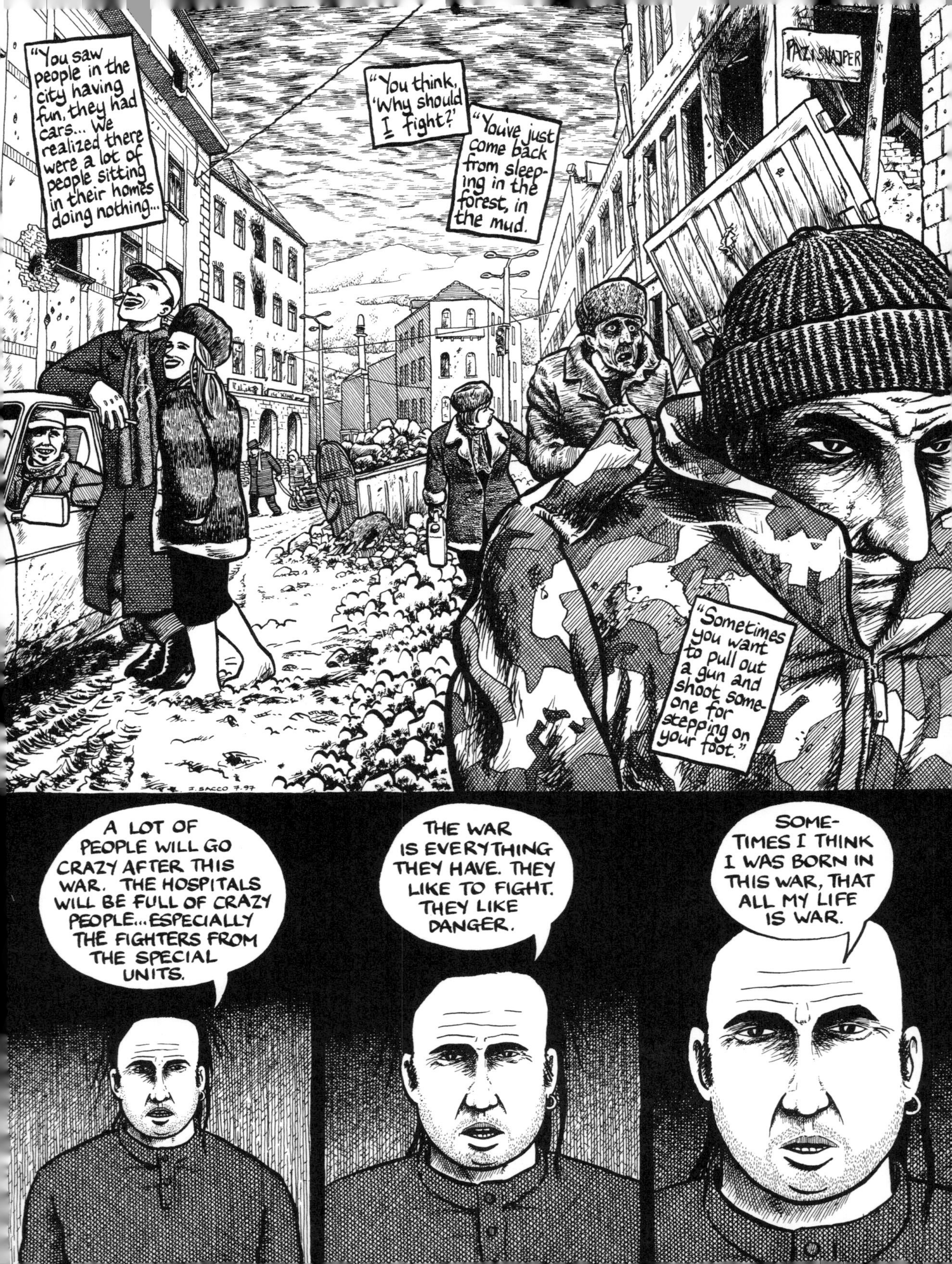
"You saw people in the city having fun, they had cars... We realized there were a lot of people sitting in their homes doing nothing...
"You think, 'Why should I fight?'
"You've just come back from sleeping in the forest, in the mud.
PAZI SNAJPER
"Sometimes you want to pull out a gun and shoot someone for stepping on your foot."
J. SACCO 7.97
A LOT OF PEOPLE WILL GO CRAZY AFTER THIS WAR. THE HOSPITALS WILL BE FULL OF CRAZY PEOPLE... ESPECIALLY THE FIGHTERS FROM THE SPECIAL UNITS.
THE WAR IS EVERYTHING THEY HAVE. THEY LIKE TO FIGHT. THEY LIKE DANGER.
SOMETIMES I THINK I WAS BORN IN THIS WAR, THAT ALL MY LIFE IS WAR.

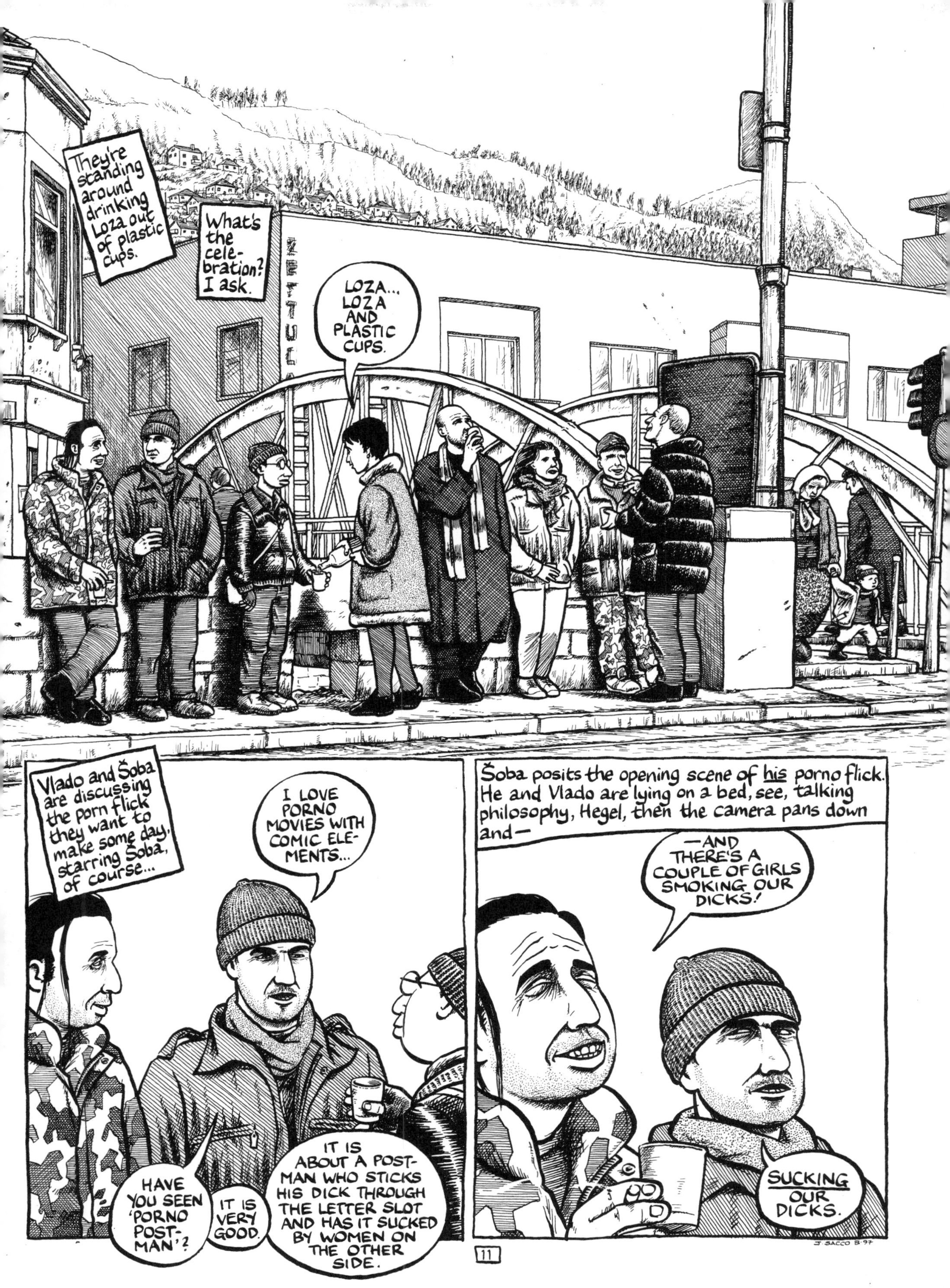

They're standing around drinking Loza out of plastic cups.
What's the celebration? I ask.
LOZA... LOZA AND PLASTIC CUPS.
ZETTULA
Vlado and Šoba are discussing the porn flick they want to make some day, starring Šoba, of course...
I LOVE PORNO MOVIES WITH COMIC ELEMENTS...
HAVE YOU SEEN 'PORNO POST-MAN'?
IT IS VERY GOOD.
IT IS ABOUT A POST-MAN WHO STICKS HIS DICK THROUGH THE LETTER SLOT AND HAS IT SUCKED BY WOMEN ON THE OTHER SIDE.
Šoba posits the opening scene of his porno flick. He and Vlado are lying on a bed, see, talking philosophy, Hegel, then the camera pans down and—
—AND THERE'S A COUPLE OF GIRLS SMOKING OUR DICKS!
SUCKING OUR DICKS.
J. SACCO 8·97

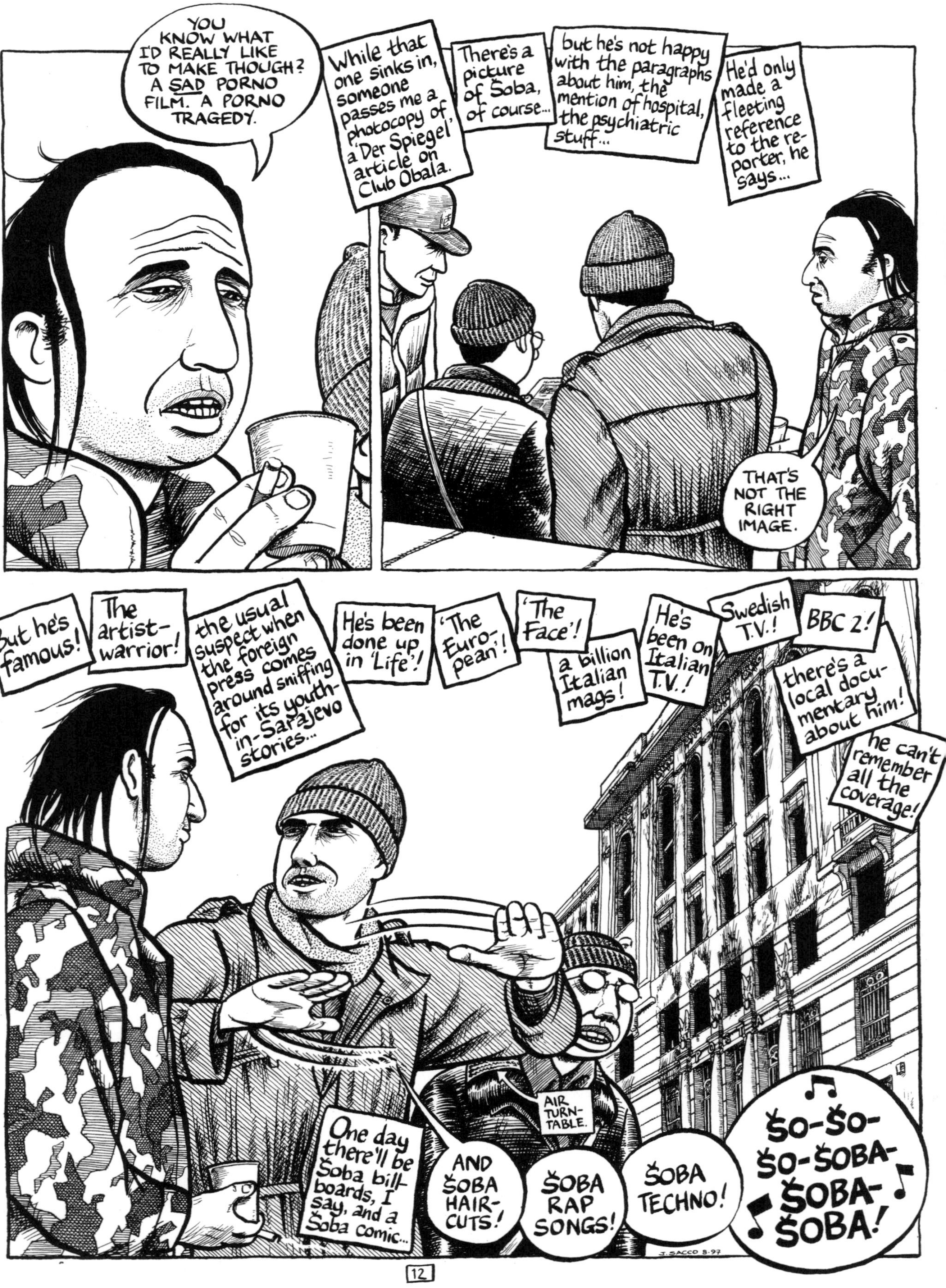

YOU KNOW WHAT I'D REALLY LIKE TO MAKE THOUGH? A SAD PORNO FILM. A PORNO TRAGEDY.
While that one sinks in, someone passes me a photocopy of a 'Der Spiegel' article on Club Obala.
There's a picture of Šoba, of course...
but he's not happy with the paragraphs about him, the mention of hospital, the psychiatric stuff...
He'd only made a fleeting reference to the reporter, he says...
THAT'S NOT THE RIGHT IMAGE.
But he's famous!
The artist-warrior!
the usual suspect when the foreign press comes around sniffing for its youth-in-Sarajevo stories...
He's been done up in 'Life'!
'The European'!
'The Face'!
a billion Italian mags!
He's been on Italian T.V.!
Swedish T.V.!
BBC 2!
there's a local documentary about him!
he can't remember all the coverage!
One day there'll be Šoba billboards, I say, and a Šoba comic...
AND ŠOBA HAIRCUTS!
AIR TURNTABLE.
ŠOBA RAP SONGS!
ŠOBA TECHNO!
ŠO-ŠO-ŠO-ŠOBA-ŠO-ŠOBA-ŠOBA-ŠOBA!
J. SACCO 8·97

LAST YEAR (1994) I HAD BIG PSYCHOLOGICAL PROBLEMS THAT DEVELOPED DURING THE CEASE-FIRE...

I FELT SO NERVOUS. THEY SAID I HAD TRAUMATIC STRESS SYN-DROME.

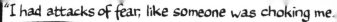

"I had attacks of fear, like someone was choking me.

"When I got out of the hospital, I couldn't sit in the trenches again...

"You can't imagine how it is in the winter. You must sit in −20°C all day and all night...

"nonstop the shells are exploding around you...

"I volunteered for land mines.

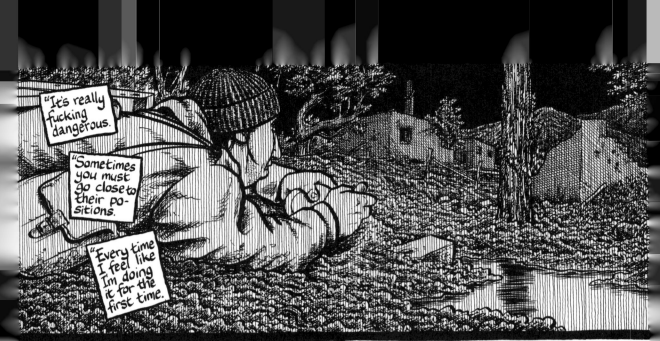

"It's really fucking dangerous.

"Sometimes you must go close to their positions.

"Every time I feel like I'm doing it for the first time.

"We are working at night... We have only a stick to find their mines...

"When we find them, we take out the explosive and replace them...They have mines that explode a mine below when you pull them out. You have to check everything...

J. SACCO 8-97

SOMETIMES I FEEL LIKE I LIKE THAT JOB. THESE DAYS I FEEL THAT THERE'S SOMETHING MISSING—LIKE I'LL GO CRAZY IF I DON'T HAVE THAT LEVEL OF INTENSITY... I'M NONSTOP IN THE ATMOSPHERE OF THAT JOB, EVEN NOW. YOU CAN'T RELAX BECAUSE YOU MUST GO BACK TO IT. I MUST KEEP THAT FEELING OR I MIGHT MAKE A MISTAKE.

I CAN'T RELAX ANYWAY. WHEN YOU RELAX YOU START THINKING, AND THEN YOU'RE THINKING, 'WHAT AM I DOING? THIS IS CRAZY.'

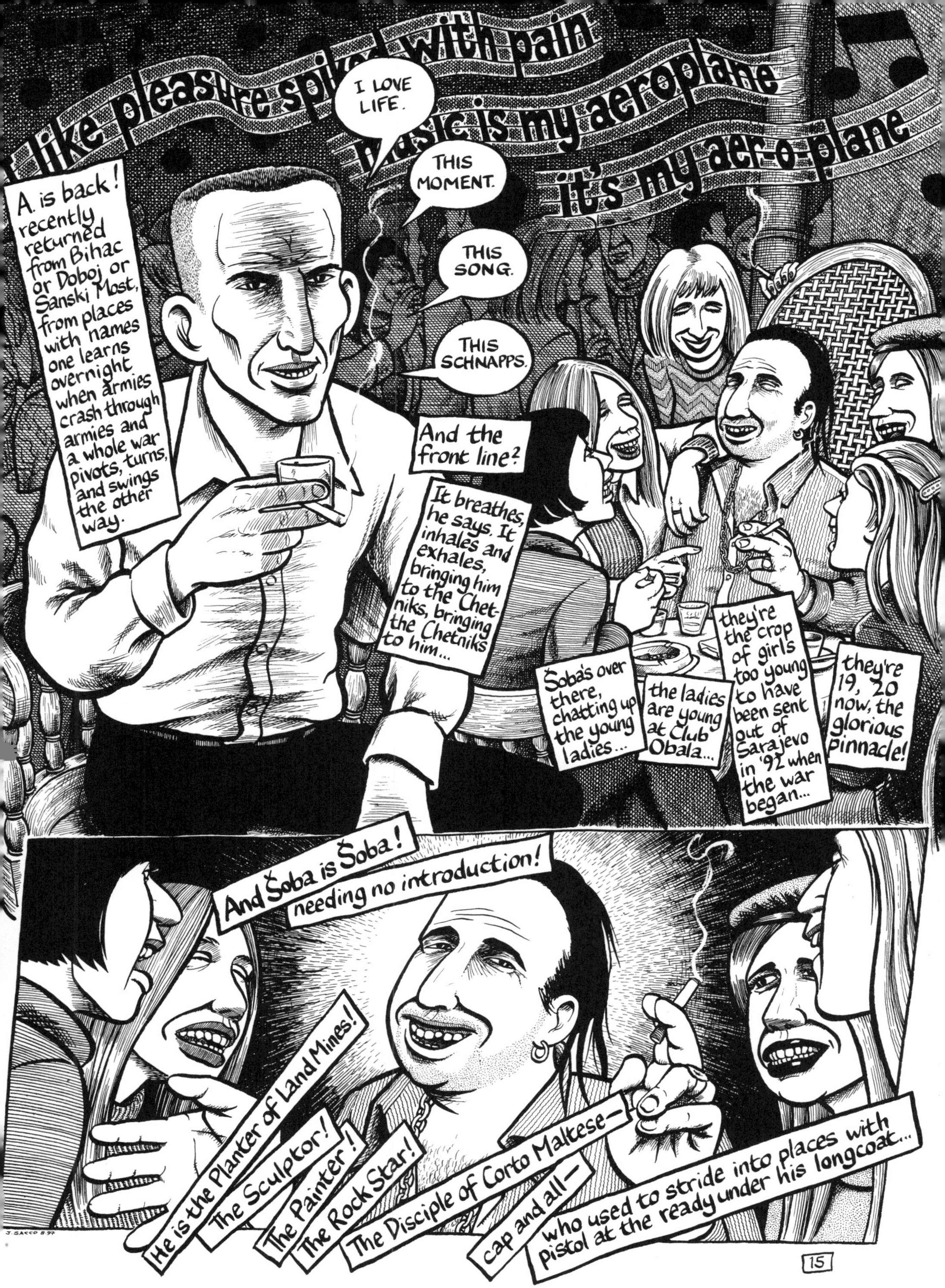
I like pleasure spiked with pain
music is my aeroplane
it's my aer-o-plane
I LOVE LIFE.
THIS MOMENT.
THIS SONG.
THIS SCHNAPPS.
A. is back! recently returned from Bihac or Doboj or Sanski Most, from places with names one learns overnight when armies crash through armies and a whole war pivots, turns, and swings the other way.
And the front line?
It breathes, he says. It inhales and exhales, bringing him to the Chetniks, bringing the Chetniks to him...
Šoba's over there, chatting up the young ladies...
the ladies are young at Club Obala...
they're the crop of girls too young to have been sent out of Sarajevo in '92 when the war began...
they're 19, 20 now, the glorious pinnacle!
And Šoba is Šoba!
needing no introduction!
He is the Planter of Land Mines!
The Sculptor!
The Painter!
The Rock Star!
The Disciple of Corto Maltese—
cap and all—
who used to stride into places with pistol at the ready under his longcoat...
J. SACCO 8.97

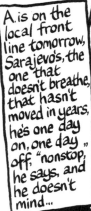

A. is on the local front line tomorrow, Sarajevo's, the one that doesn't breathe, that hasn't moved in years, he's one day on, one day off, "nonstop," he says, and he doesn't mind...

Anyway, the cease-fire is holding, he thinks the war is over...

I AM ALIVE.

I AM HERE.

His best friends are dead, both brothers killed in action, his mother and other family massacred, and you don't know the half of it...he himself is what people here call a Great Fighter...he is special units, wounded in four places...

One day he showed me the bullet marks in his armored jacket.

I AM THE BEST.

I DON'T KNOW WHAT FEAR IS.

JOE!

I LIKE PLEASURE SPIKED WITH PAIN, MUSIC IS MY AEROPLANE...

IT'S MY AER-O-PLANE...

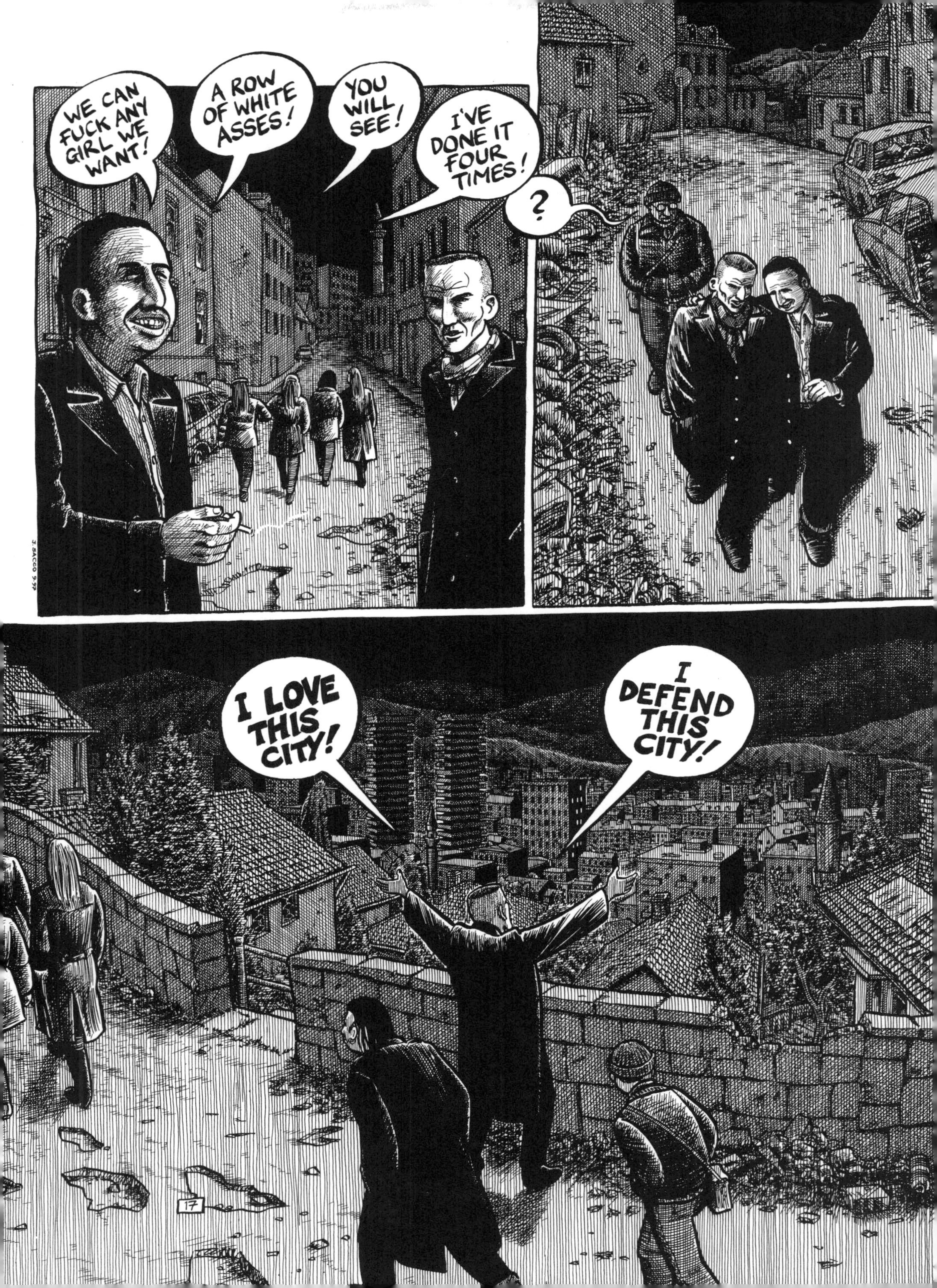
WE CAN FUCK ANY GIRL WE WANT!
A ROW OF WHITE ASSES!
YOU WILL SEE!
I'VE DONE IT FOUR TIMES!
?
J. SACCO 9.97
I LOVE THIS CITY!
I DEFEND THIS CITY!

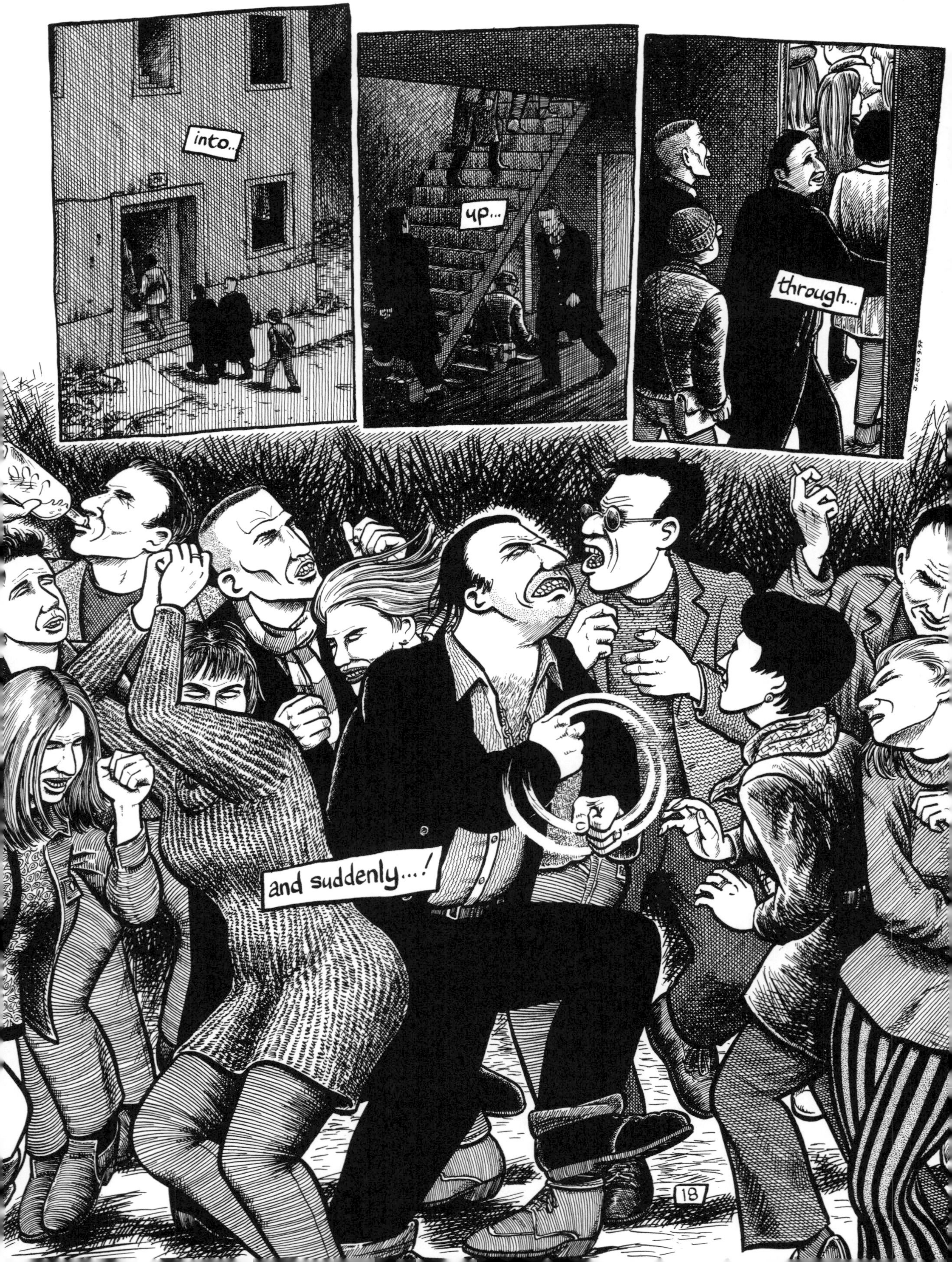
into..
up...
through...
and suddenly....!
J. SACCO 9.97

Šoba!
He's surrounded a cutie!
He's putting on incredible moves!
working on her!
dancing trashy!
bumping!
grinding!
Travoltaing in a way that'd drop an ordinary chick to her knees!

Not her though.

The Planter of Land Mines, who had to hang on to the roots of trees during the artillery barrages on Žuč, can barely get a wiggle out of her bottoms!

Now A. lends his ass... The Great Fighter and the Planter of Land Mines are introducing coordinated dance moves and playing the homoerotic card to get her messy, but no dice!

The boys take off their long-coats... Šoba even strips off his 1972 Pierre Cordin shirt... It's getting serious now, but where's Little Miss Bubblegum?

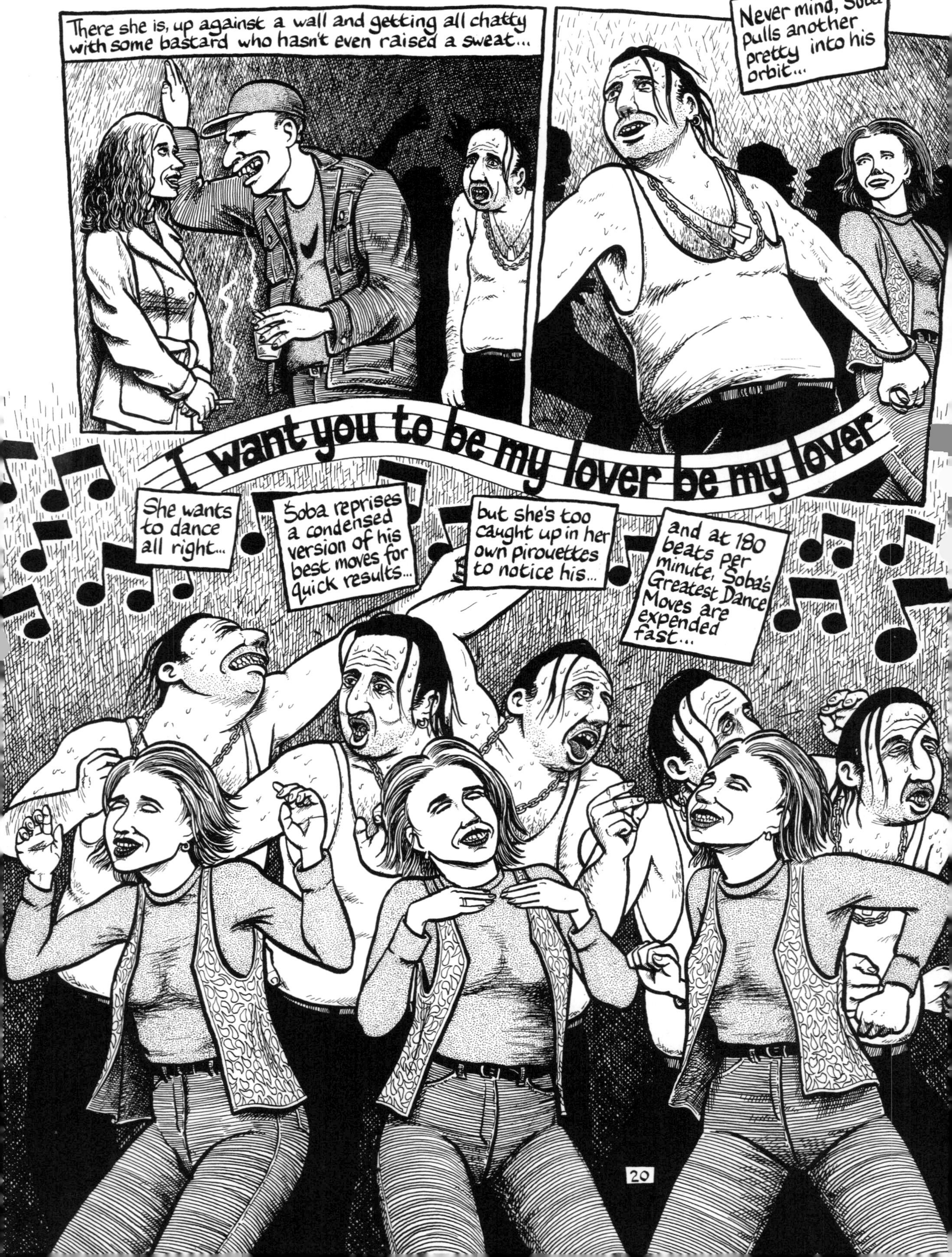
There she is, up against a wall and getting all chatty with some bastard who hasn't even raised a sweat...
Never mind, Šoba pulls another pretty into his orbit...
I want you to be my lover be my lover
She wants to dance all right...
Šoba reprises a condensed version of his best moves for quick results...
but she's too caught up in her own pirouettes to notice his...
and at 180 beats per minute, Šoba's Greatest Dance Moves are expended fast...

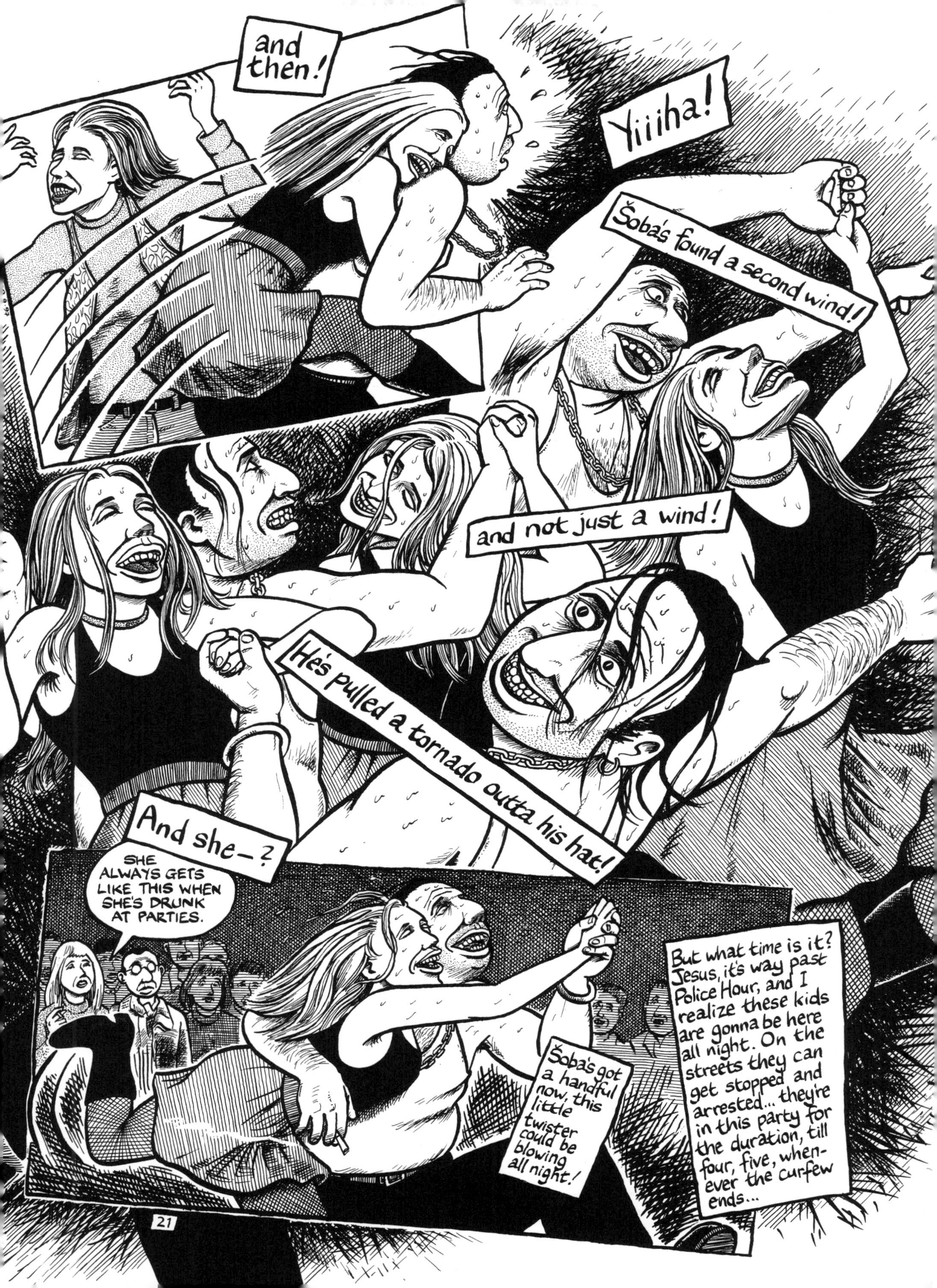

and then!
Yiiiha!
Šoba's found a second wind!
and not just a wind!
He's pulled a tornado outta his hat!
And she–?
SHE ALWAYS GETS LIKE THIS WHEN SHE'S DRUNK AT PARTIES.
Šoba's got a handful now, this little twister could be blowing all night!
But what time is it? Jesus, it's way past Police Hour, and I realize these kids are gonna be here all night. On the streets they can get stopped and arrested... they're in this party for the duration, till four, five, whenever the curfew ends...

I've got U.N. credentials, a Blue Card, if the police stop me, I'll flash 'em that...

But it's not the police I'm worried about.

It's the rustling in the garbage, it's the growling.

It's the soft trotting behind you that stops every time you stop.

It's the dogs.

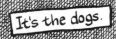

22

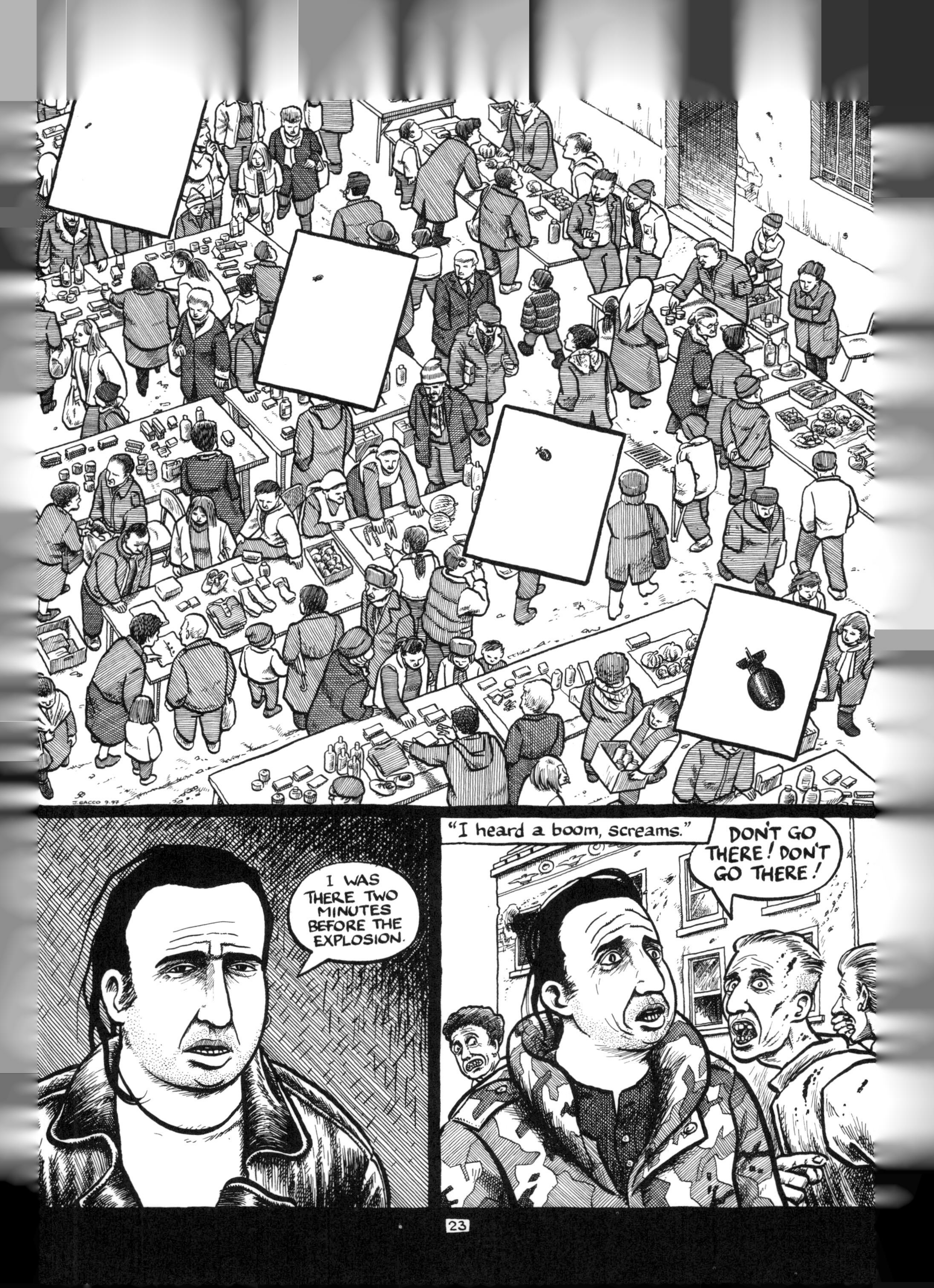
J. SACCO 9.97
I WAS THERE TWO MINUTES BEFORE THE EXPLOSION.
"I heard a boom, screams."
DON'T GO THERE! DON'T GO THERE!

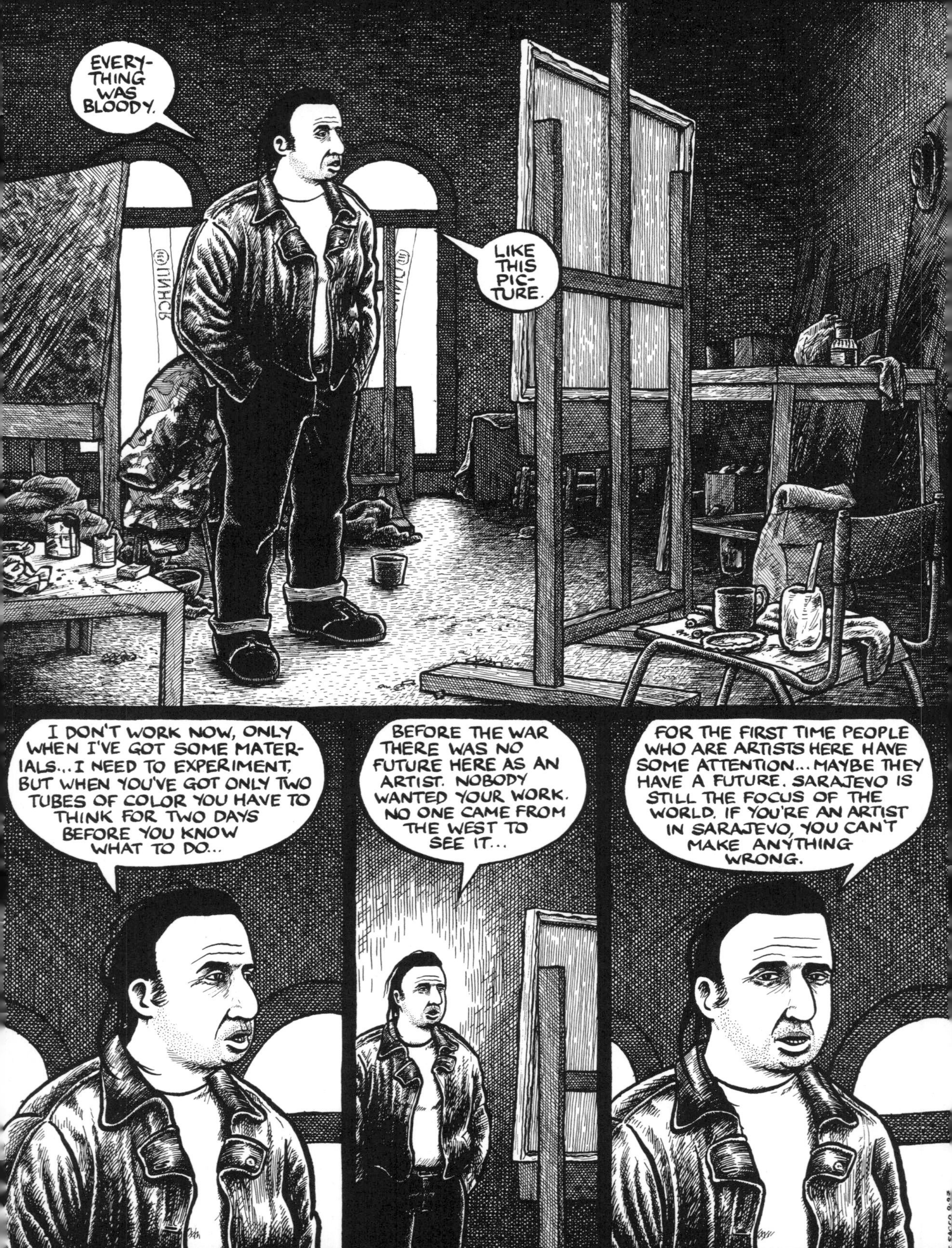

EVERYTHING WAS BLOODY.
LIKE THIS PICTURE.
I DON'T WORK NOW, ONLY WHEN I'VE GOT SOME MATERIALS... I NEED TO EXPERIMENT, BUT WHEN YOU'VE GOT ONLY TWO TUBES OF COLOR YOU HAVE TO THINK FOR TWO DAYS BEFORE YOU KNOW WHAT TO DO...
BEFORE THE WAR THERE WAS NO FUTURE HERE AS AN ARTIST. NOBODY WANTED YOUR WORK. NO ONE CAME FROM THE WEST TO SEE IT...
FOR THE FIRST TIME PEOPLE WHO ARE ARTISTS HERE HAVE SOME ATTENTION... MAYBE THEY HAVE A FUTURE. SARAJEVO IS STILL THE FOCUS OF THE WORLD. IF YOU'RE AN ARTIST IN SARAJEVO, YOU CAN'T MAKE ANYTHING WRONG.

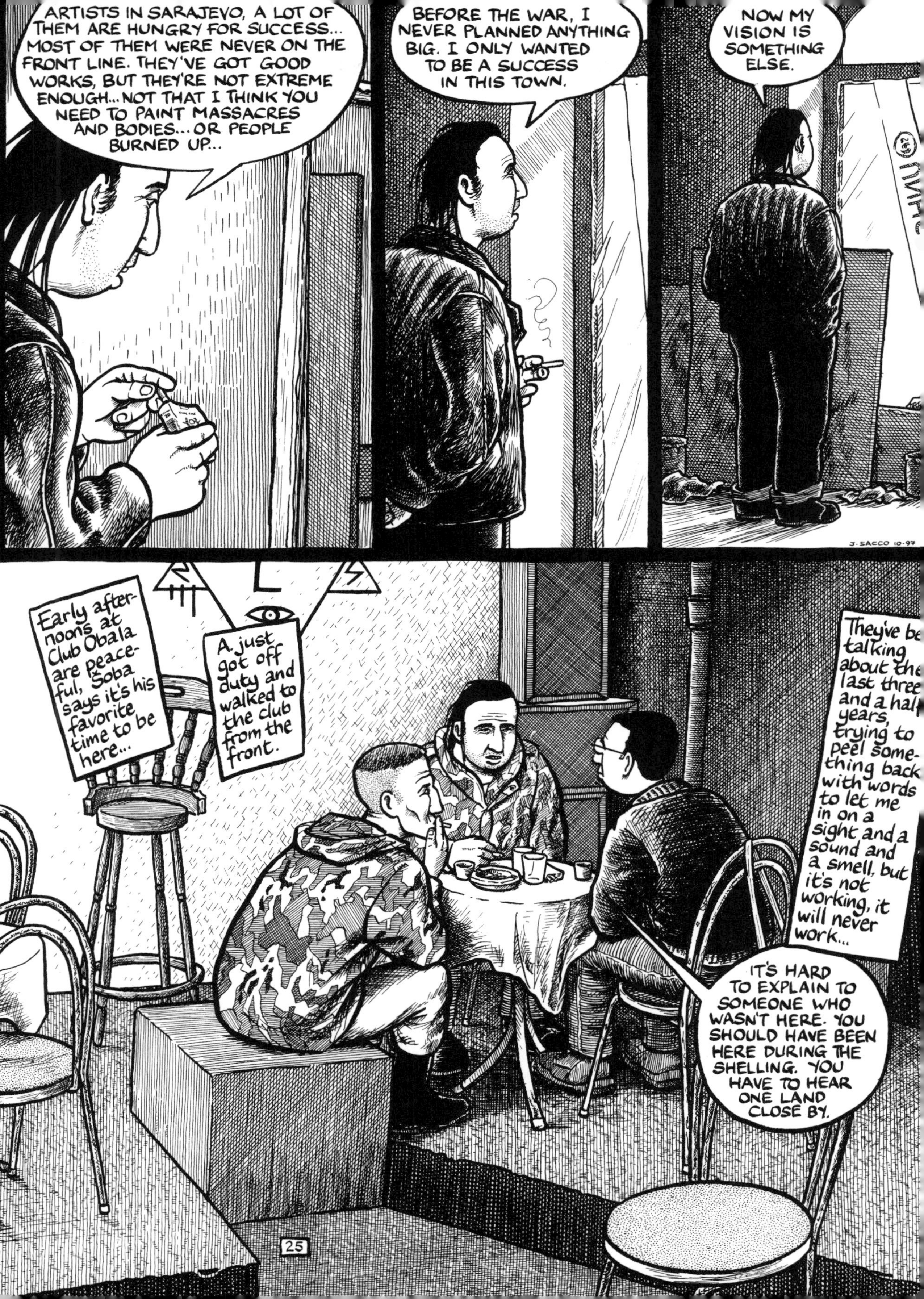
ARTISTS IN SARAJEVO, A LOT OF THEM ARE HUNGRY FOR SUCCESS... MOST OF THEM WERE NEVER ON THE FRONT LINE. THEY'VE GOT GOOD WORKS, BUT THEY'RE NOT EXTREME ENOUGH... NOT THAT I THINK YOU NEED TO PAINT MASSACRES AND BODIES... OR PEOPLE BURNED UP...
BEFORE THE WAR, I NEVER PLANNED ANYTHING BIG. I ONLY WANTED TO BE A SUCCESS IN THIS TOWN.
NOW MY VISION IS SOMETHING ELSE.
J. SACCO 10-97
Early afternoons at Club Obala are peaceful, Šoba says it's his favorite time to be here...
A. just got off duty and walked to the club from the front.
They've be talking about the last three and a hal years, trying to peel something back with words to let me in on a sight and a sound and a smell, but it's not working, it will never work...
IT'S HARD TO EXPLAIN TO SOMEONE WHO WASN'T HERE. YOU SHOULD HAVE BEEN HERE DURING THE SHELLING. YOU HAVE TO HEAR ONE LAND CLOSE BY.

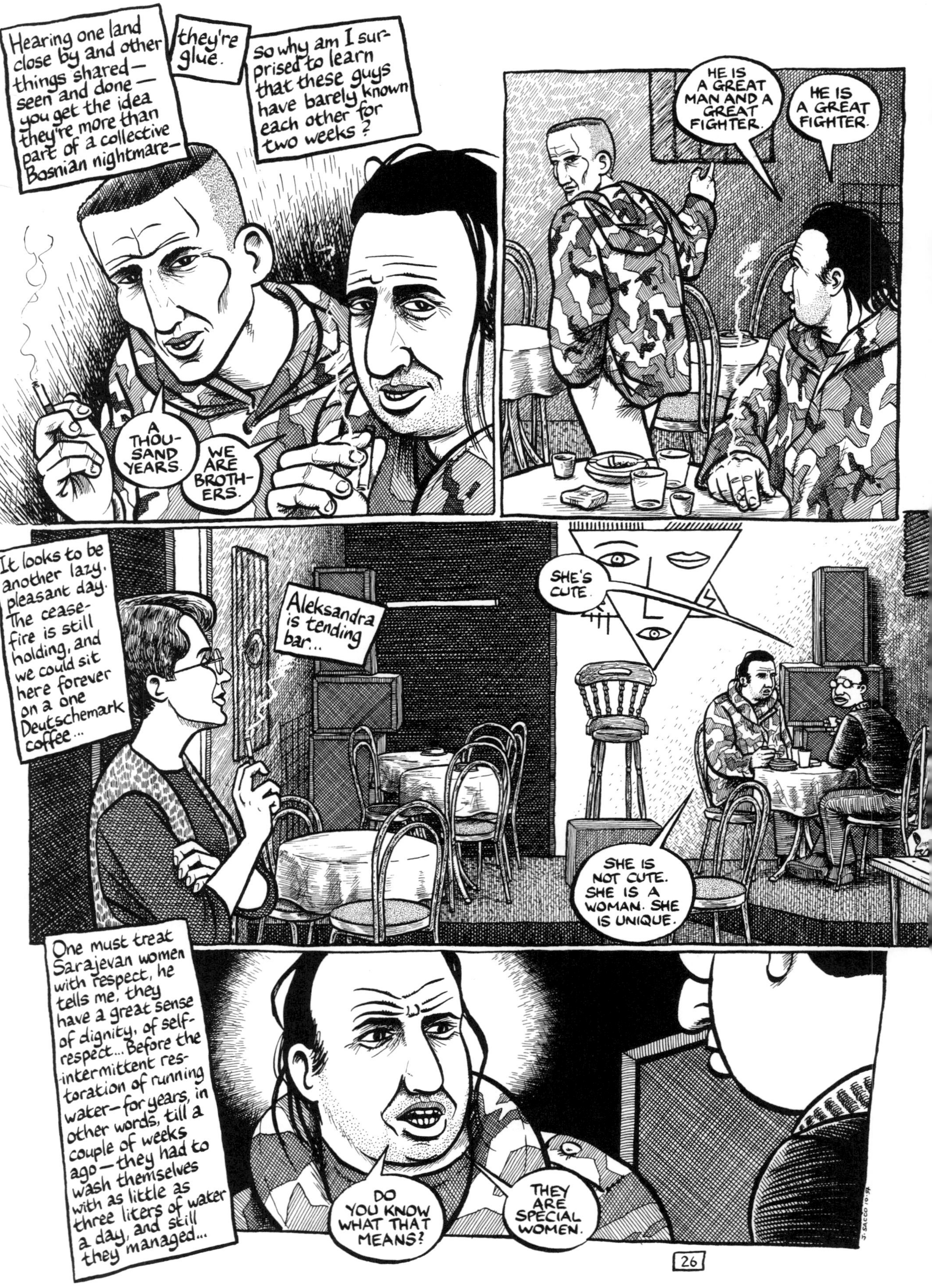

Hearing one land close by and other things shared—seen and done—you get the idea they're more than part of a collective Bosnian nightmare—
they're glue.
So why am I surprised to learn that these guys have barely known each other for two weeks?
A THOUSAND YEARS.
WE ARE BROTHERS.
HE IS A GREAT MAN AND A GREAT FIGHTER.
HE IS A GREAT FIGHTER.
It looks to be another lazy, pleasant day. The cease-fire is still holding, and we could sit here forever on a one Deutschemark coffee...
Aleksandra is tending bar...
SHE'S CUTE.
SHE IS NOT CUTE. SHE IS A WOMAN. SHE IS UNIQUE.
One must treat Sarajevan women with respect, he tells me, they have a great sense of dignity, of self-respect... Before the intermittent restoration of running water—for years, in other words, till a couple of weeks ago—they had to wash themselves with as little as three liters of water a day, and still they managed...
DO YOU KNOW WHAT THAT MEANS?
THEY ARE SPECIAL WOMEN.

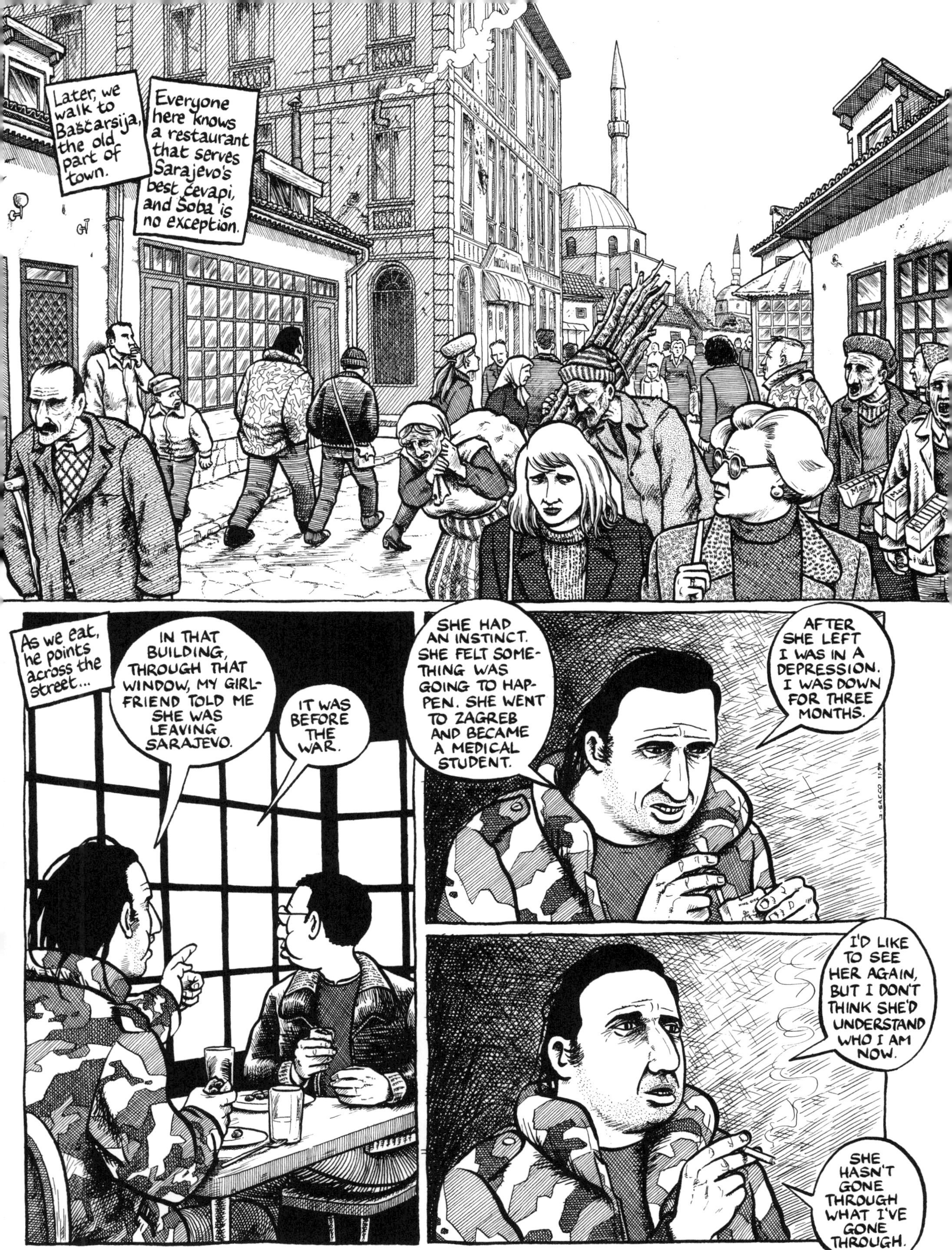
Later, we walk to Baščaršija, the old part of town.
Everyone here knows a restaurant that serves Sarajevo's best ćevapi, and Šoba is no exception.
As we eat, he points across the street...
IN THAT BUILDING, THROUGH THAT WINDOW, MY GIRLFRIEND TOLD ME SHE WAS LEAVING SARAJEVO.
IT WAS BEFORE THE WAR.
SHE HAD AN INSTINCT. SHE FELT SOMETHING WAS GOING TO HAPPEN. SHE WENT TO ZAGREB AND BECAME A MEDICAL STUDENT.
AFTER SHE LEFT I WAS IN A DEPRESSION. I WAS DOWN FOR THREE MONTHS.
I'D LIKE TO SEE HER AGAIN, BUT I DON'T THINK SHE'D UNDERSTAND WHO I AM NOW.
SHE HASN'T GONE THROUGH WHAT I'VE GONE THROUGH.

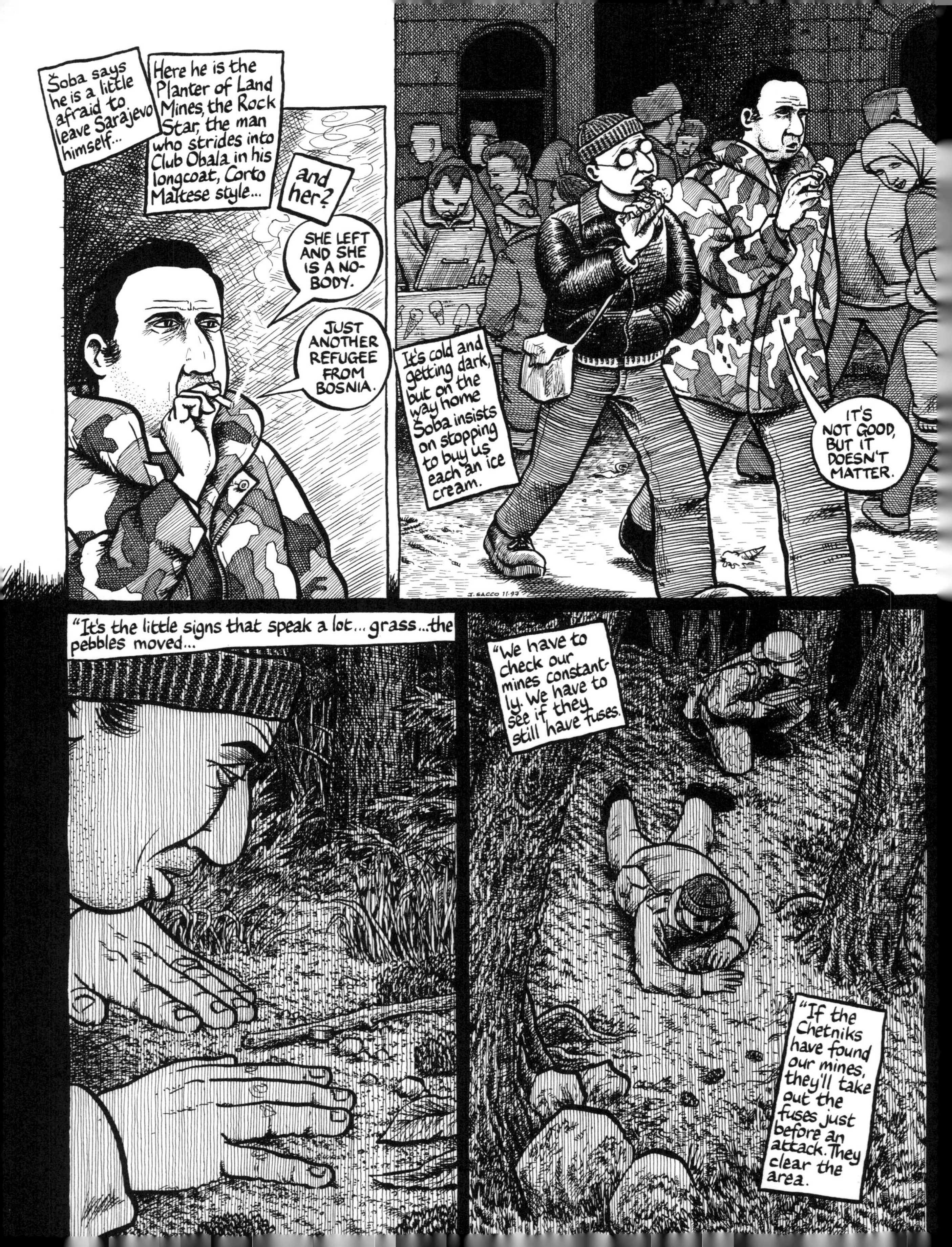
Šoba says he is a little afraid to leave Sarajevo himself...
Here he is the Planter of Land Mines, the Rock Star, the man who strides into Club Obala in his longcoat, Corto Maltese style...
and her?
SHE LEFT AND SHE IS A NO-BODY.
JUST ANOTHER REFUGEE FROM BOSNIA.
It's cold and getting dark, but on the way home Šoba insists on stopping to buy us each an ice cream.
IT'S NOT GOOD, BUT IT DOESN'T MATTER.
J. SACCO 11·97
"It's the little signs that speak a lot... grass... the pebbles moved...
"We have to check our mines constantly. We have to see if they still have fuses.
"If the Chetniks have found our mines, they'll take out the fuses just before an attack. They clear the area.

"The enemy has new mines now, Russian ones, they're big and black. There's only one guy in town who knows how to disarm those mines. He'll teach the rest of us.

"Recently we were clearing an old minefield. The best guy in my unit stood up and tripped a mine, but he only lost the heel of his boot."

THEN TWO DAYS AGO ONE OF MY FRIENDS LOST HIS LEG ON A MINE.

I run into Soba at the Billiard Club...

Tomorrow night has got him jittery.

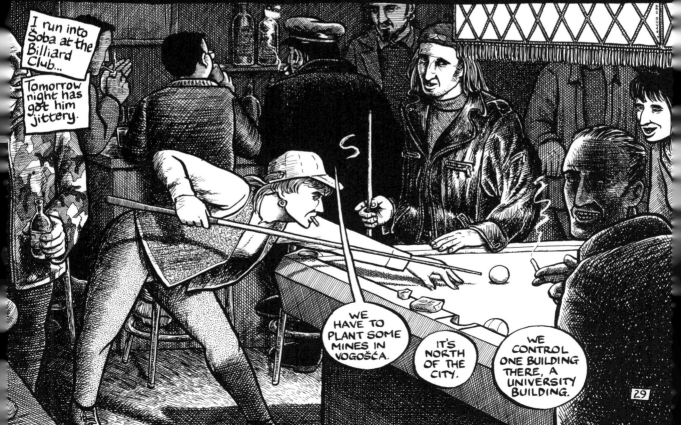

WE HAVE TO PLANT SOME MINES IN VOGOŚĆA.

IT'S NORTH OF THE CITY.

WE CONTROL ONE BUILDING THERE, A UNIVERSITY BUILDING.

29

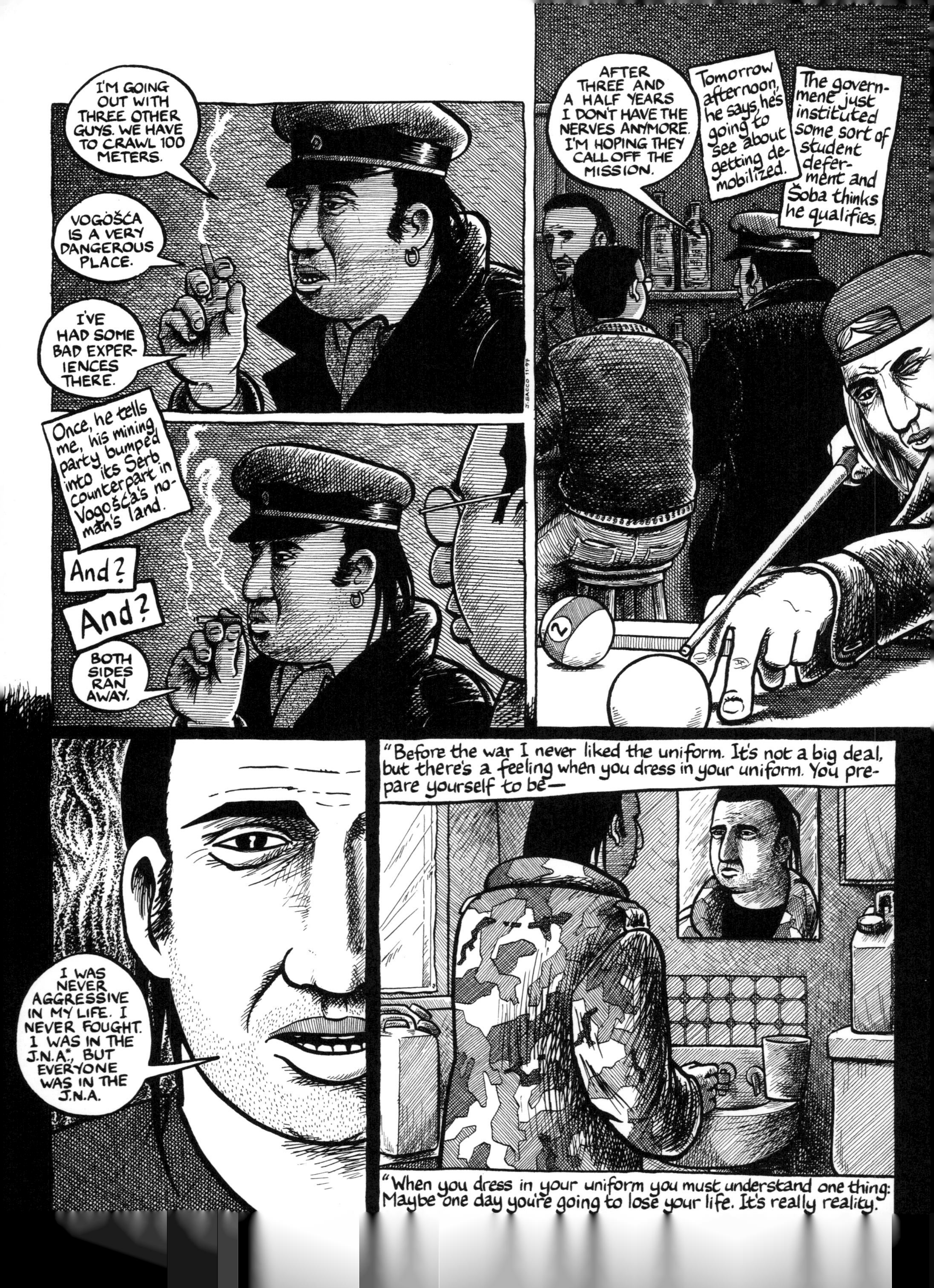
I'M GOING OUT WITH THREE OTHER GUYS. WE HAVE TO CRAWL 100 METERS.
VOGOŠĆA IS A VERY DANGEROUS PLACE.
I'VE HAD SOME BAD EXPERIENCES THERE.
J. SACCO 11-97
Once, he tells me, his mining party bumped into its Serb counterpart in Vogošća's no-man's land.
And?
And?
BOTH SIDES RAN AWAY.
AFTER THREE AND A HALF YEARS I DON'T HAVE THE NERVES ANYMORE. I'M HOPING THEY CALL OFF THE MISSION.
Tomorrow afternoon, he says, he's going to see about getting de-mobilized.
The government just instituted some sort of student deferment and Šoba thinks he qualifies.
2
I WAS NEVER AGGRESSIVE IN MY LIFE. I NEVER FOUGHT. I WAS IN THE J.N.A.*, BUT EVERYONE WAS IN THE J.N.A.
"Before the war I never liked the uniform. It's not a big deal, but there's a feeling when you dress in your uniform. You prepare yourself to be—
"When you dress in your uniform you must understand one thing: Maybe one day you're going to lose your life. It's really reality.

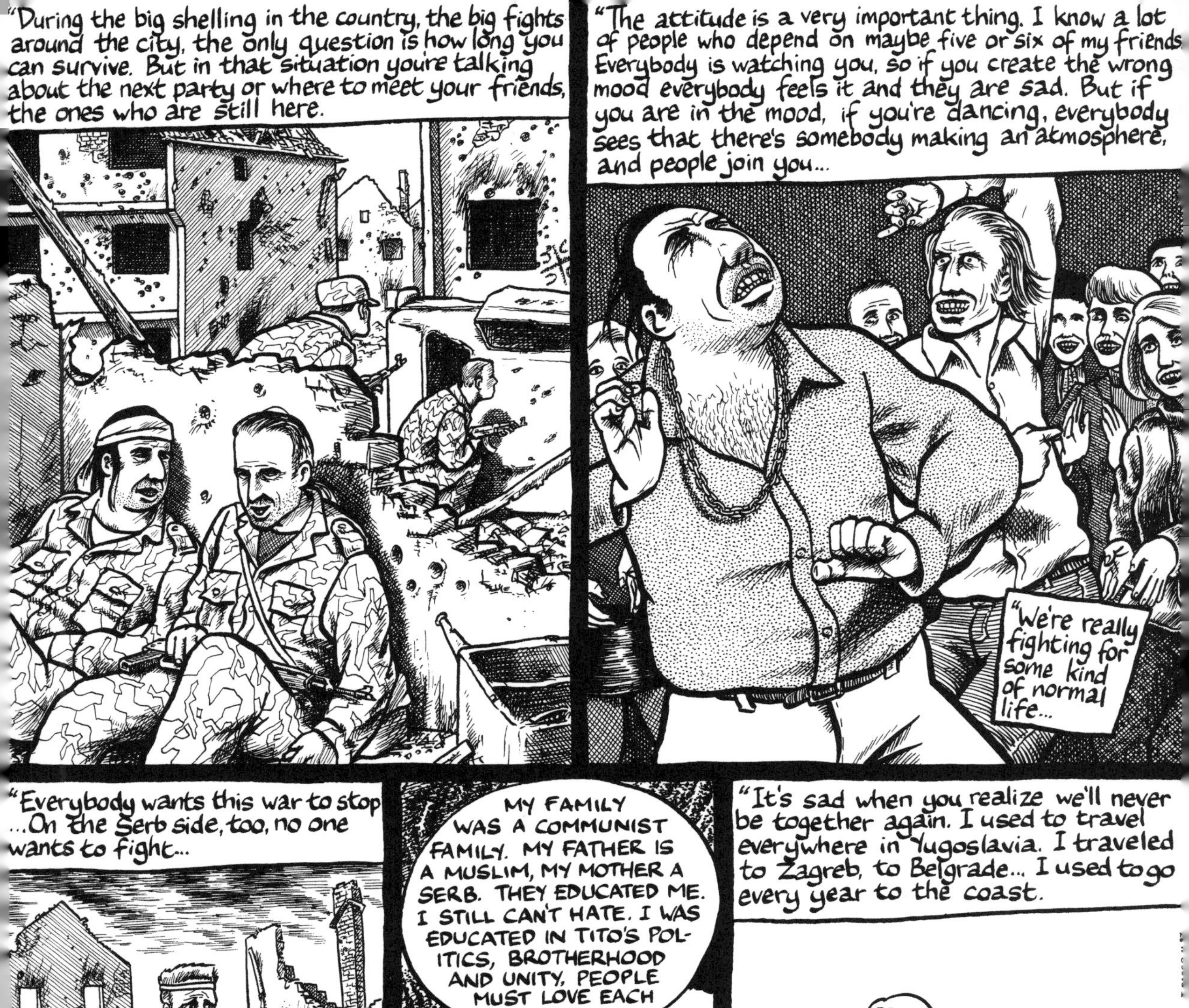
"During the big shelling in the country, the big fights around the city, the only question is how long you can survive. But in that situation youre talking about the next party or where to meet your friends, the ones who are still here.
"The attitude is a very important thing. I know a lot of people who depend on maybe five or six of my friends. Everybody is watching you, so if you create the wrong mood everybody feels it and they are sad. But if you are in the mood, if you're dancing, everybody sees that there's somebody making an atmosphere, and people join you...
"We're really fighting for some kind of normal life...
"Everybody wants this war to stop ...On the Serb side, too, no one wants to fight...
"The people were so mixed. I think we've all lost this war. Maybe Croatia profited from this war."
MY FAMILY WAS A COMMUNIST FAMILY. MY FATHER IS A MUSLIM, MY MOTHER A SERB. THEY EDUCATED ME. I STILL CAN'T HATE. I WAS EDUCATED IN TITO'S POLITICS, BROTHERHOOD AND UNITY, PEOPLE MUST LOVE EACH OTHER.
"It's sad when you realize we'll never be together again. I used to travel everywhere in Yugoslavia. I traveled to Zagreb, to Belgrade... I used to go every year to the coast.

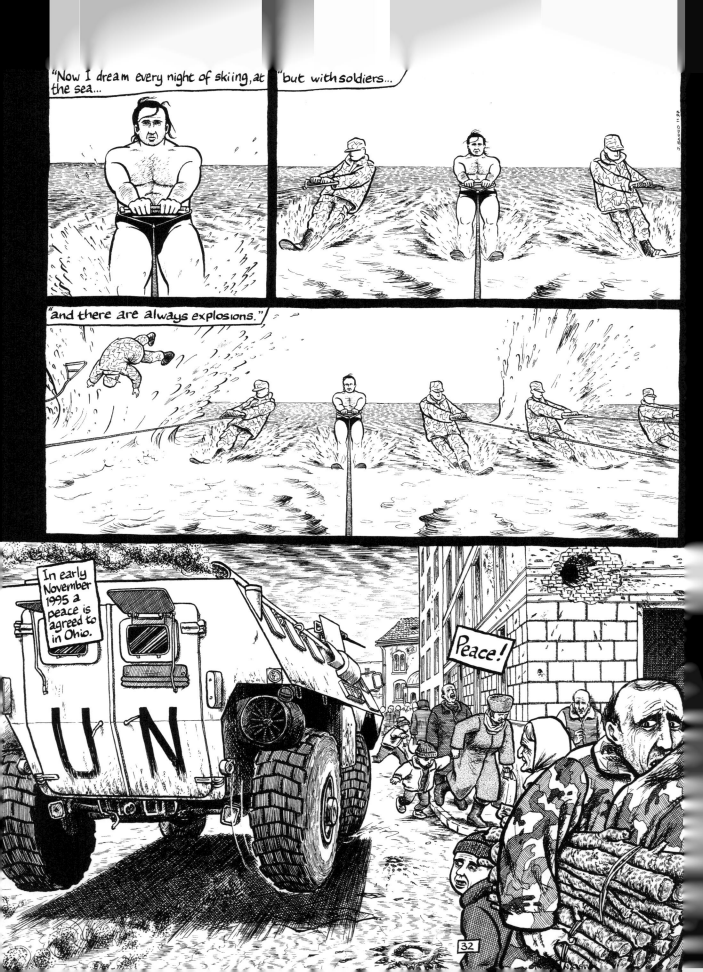

"Now I dream every night of skiing, at the sea...

"but with soldiers...

"and there are always explosions."

In early November 1995 a peace is agreed to in Ohio.

UN

Peace!

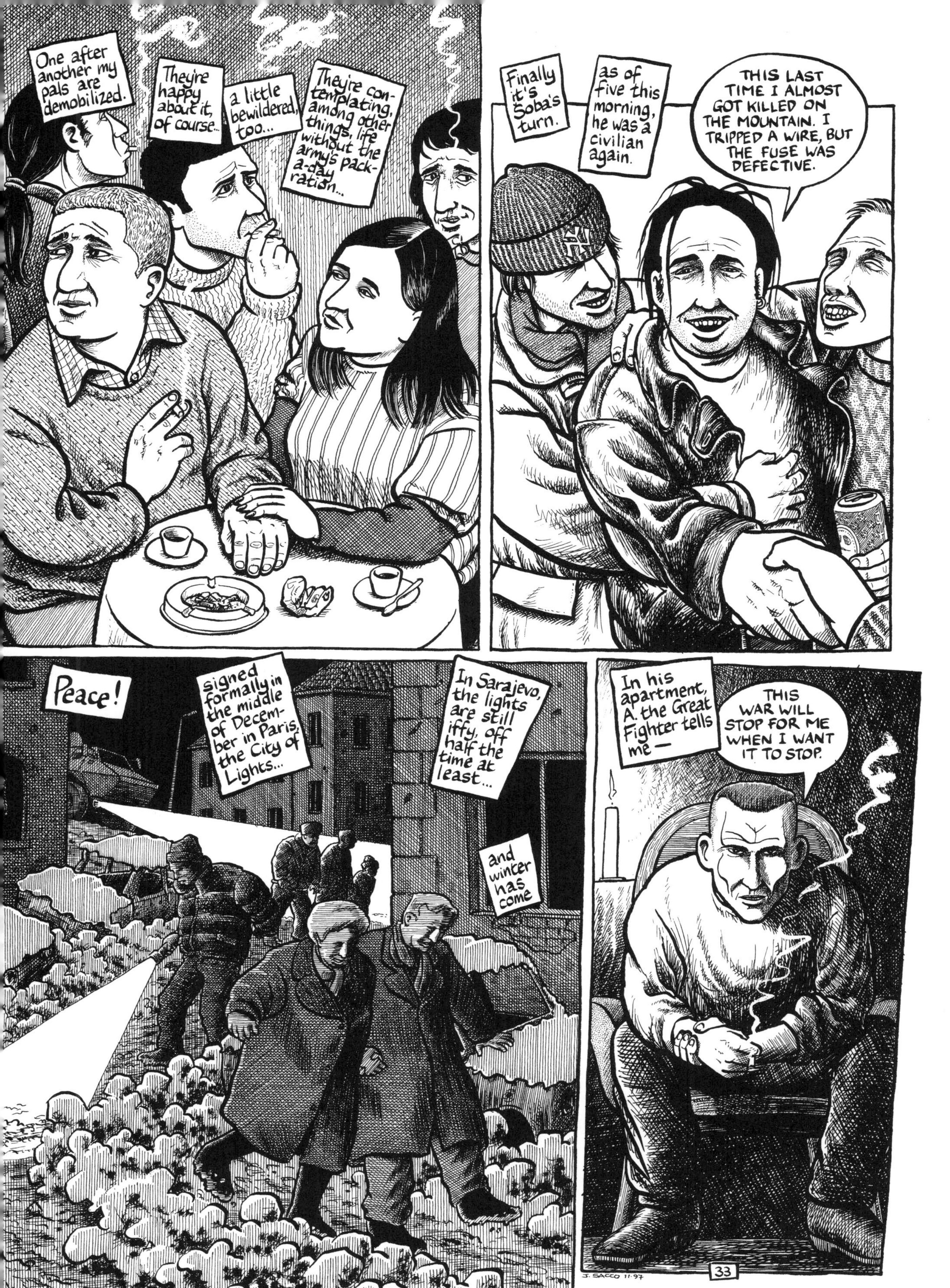
One after another my pals are demobilized.
They're happy about it, of course...
a little bewildered, too...
They're contemplating, among other things, life without the army's pack-a-day ration...
Finally it's Šoba's turn.
as of five this morning, he was a civilian again.
THIS LAST TIME I ALMOST GOT KILLED ON THE MOUNTAIN. I TRIPPED A WIRE, BUT THE FUSE WAS DEFECTIVE.
Peace!
signed formally in the middle of December in Paris, the City of Lights...
In Sarajevo, the lights are still iffy, off half the time at least...
and winter has come
In his apartment, A. the Great Fighter tells me—
THIS WAR WILL STOP FOR ME WHEN I WANT IT TO STOP.
J. SACCO 11·97

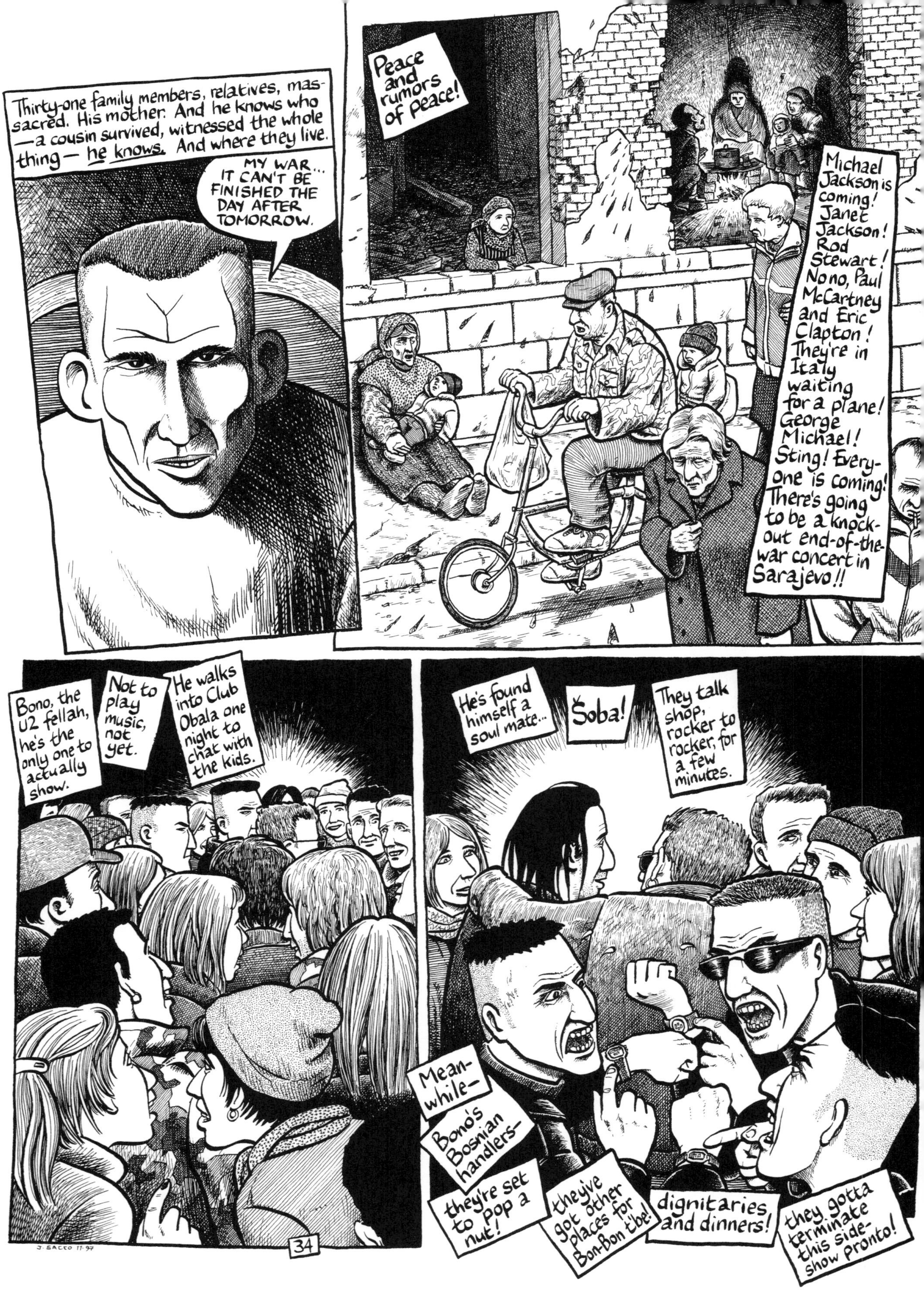

Thirty-one family members, relatives, massacred. His mother. And he knows who—a cousin survived, witnessed the whole thing— he knows. And where they live.
MY WAR... IT CAN'T BE FINISHED THE DAY AFTER TOMORROW.
Peace and rumors of peace!
Michael Jackson is coming! Janet Jackson! Rod Stewart! No no, Paul McCartney and Eric Clapton! They're in Italy waiting for a plane! George Michael! Sting! Everyone is coming! There's going to be a knock-out end-of-the-war concert in Sarajevo!!
Bono, the U2 fellah, he's the only one to actually show.
Not to play music, not yet.
He walks into Club Obala one night to chat with the kids.
He's found himself a soul mate...
Šoba!
They talk shop, rocker to rocker, for a few minutes.
Meanwhile—
Bono's Bosnian handlers—
they're set to pop a nut!
they've got other places for Bon-Bon t'be!
dignitaries and dinners!
they gotta terminate this side-show pronto!
J. SACCO 11·97

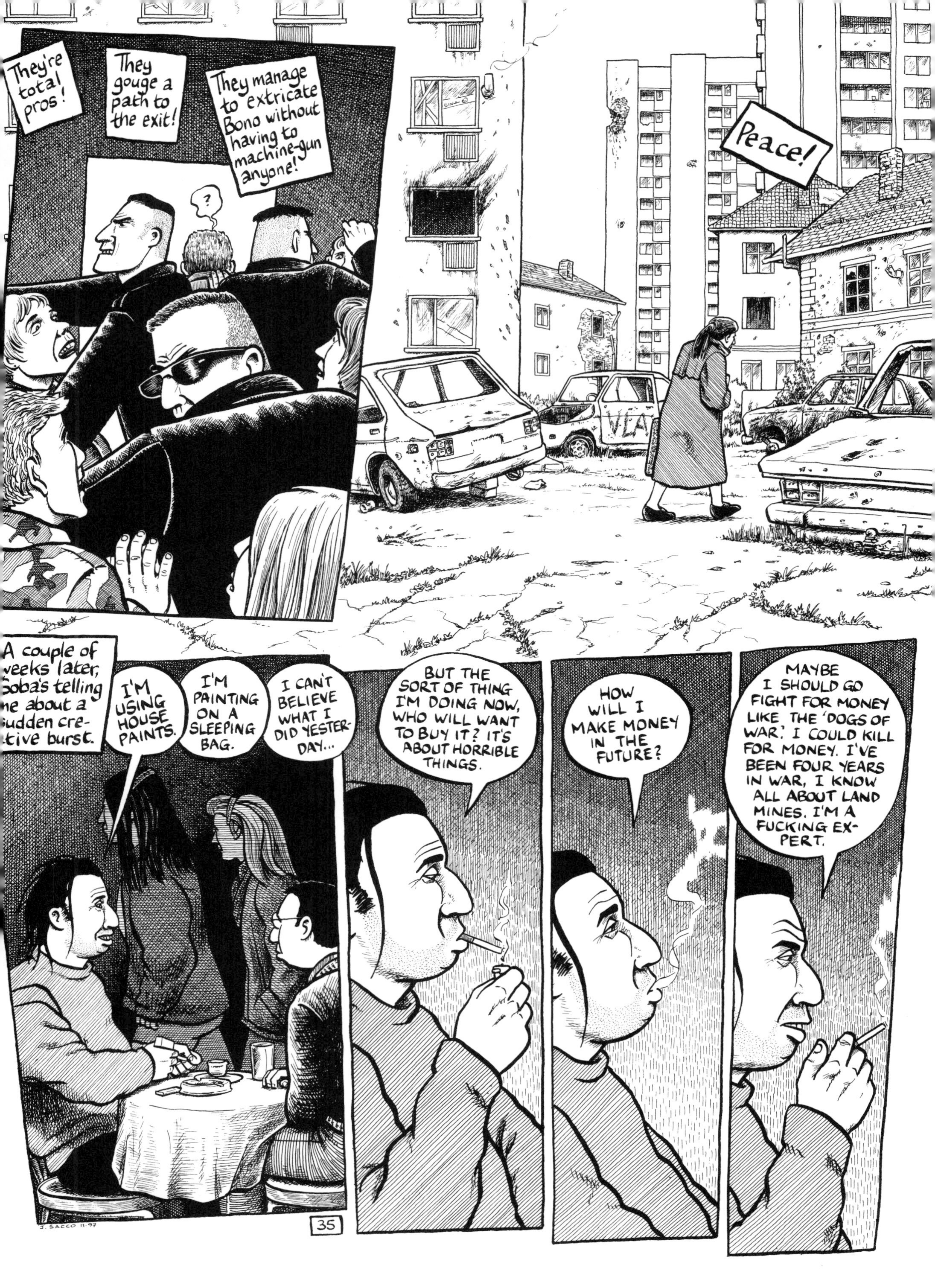
They're total pros!
They gouge a path to the exit!
They manage to extricate Bono without having to machine-gun anyone!
?
Peace!
A couple of veeks later, Soba's telling ne about a udden cre- tive burst.
I'M USING HOUSE PAINTS.
I'M PAINTING ON A SLEEPING BAG.
I CAN'T BELIEVE WHAT I DID YESTER-DAY...
BUT THE SORT OF THING I'M DOING NOW, WHO WILL WANT TO BUY IT? IT'S ABOUT HORRIBLE THINGS.
HOW WILL I MAKE MONEY IN THE FUTURE?
MAYBE I SHOULD GO FIGHT FOR MONEY LIKE THE 'DOGS OF WAR.' I COULD KILL FOR MONEY. I'VE BEEN FOUR YEARS IN WAR, I KNOW ALL ABOUT LAND MINES. I'M A FUCKING EX-PERT.
J. SACCO 11.97

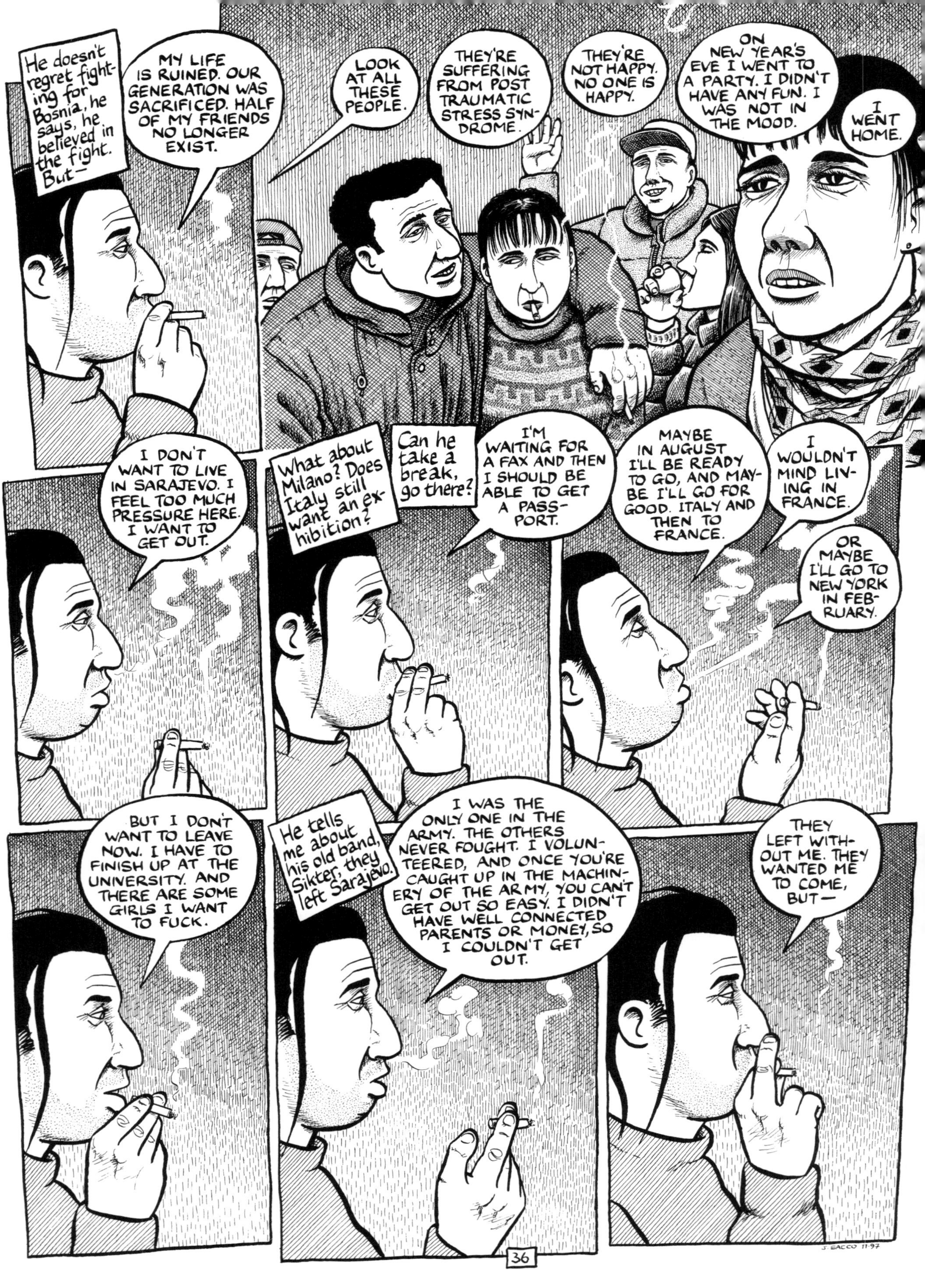
He doesn't regret fighting for Bosnia, he says, he believed in the fight. But—
MY LIFE IS RUINED. OUR GENERATION WAS SACRIFICED. HALF OF MY FRIENDS NO LONGER EXIST.
LOOK AT ALL THESE PEOPLE.
THEY'RE SUFFERING FROM POST TRAUMATIC STRESS SYNDROME.
THEY'RE NOT HAPPY. NO ONE IS HAPPY.
ON NEW YEAR'S EVE I WENT TO A PARTY. I DIDN'T HAVE ANY FUN. I WAS NOT IN THE MOOD.
I WENT HOME.
I DON'T WANT TO LIVE IN SARAJEVO. I FEEL TOO MUCH PRESSURE HERE. I WANT TO GET OUT.
What about Milano? Does Italy still want an exhibition?
Can he take a break, go there?
I'M WAITING FOR A FAX AND THEN I SHOULD BE ABLE TO GET A PASSPORT.
MAYBE IN AUGUST I'LL BE READY TO GO, AND MAYBE I'LL GO FOR GOOD. ITALY AND THEN TO FRANCE.
I WOULDN'T MIND LIVING IN FRANCE.
OR MAYBE I'LL GO TO NEW YORK IN FEBRUARY.
BUT I DON'T WANT TO LEAVE NOW. I HAVE TO FINISH UP AT THE UNIVERSITY. AND THERE ARE SOME GIRLS I WANT TO FUCK.
He tells me about his old band, Sikter, they left Sarajevo.
I WAS THE ONLY ONE IN THE ARMY. THE OTHERS NEVER FOUGHT. I VOLUNTEERED, AND ONCE YOU'RE CAUGHT UP IN THE MACHINERY OF THE ARMY, YOU CAN'T GET OUT SO EASY. I DIDN'T HAVE WELL CONNECTED PARENTS OR MONEY, SO I COULDN'T GET OUT.
THEY LEFT WITHOUT ME. THEY WANTED ME TO COME, BUT—
J. SACCO 11-97

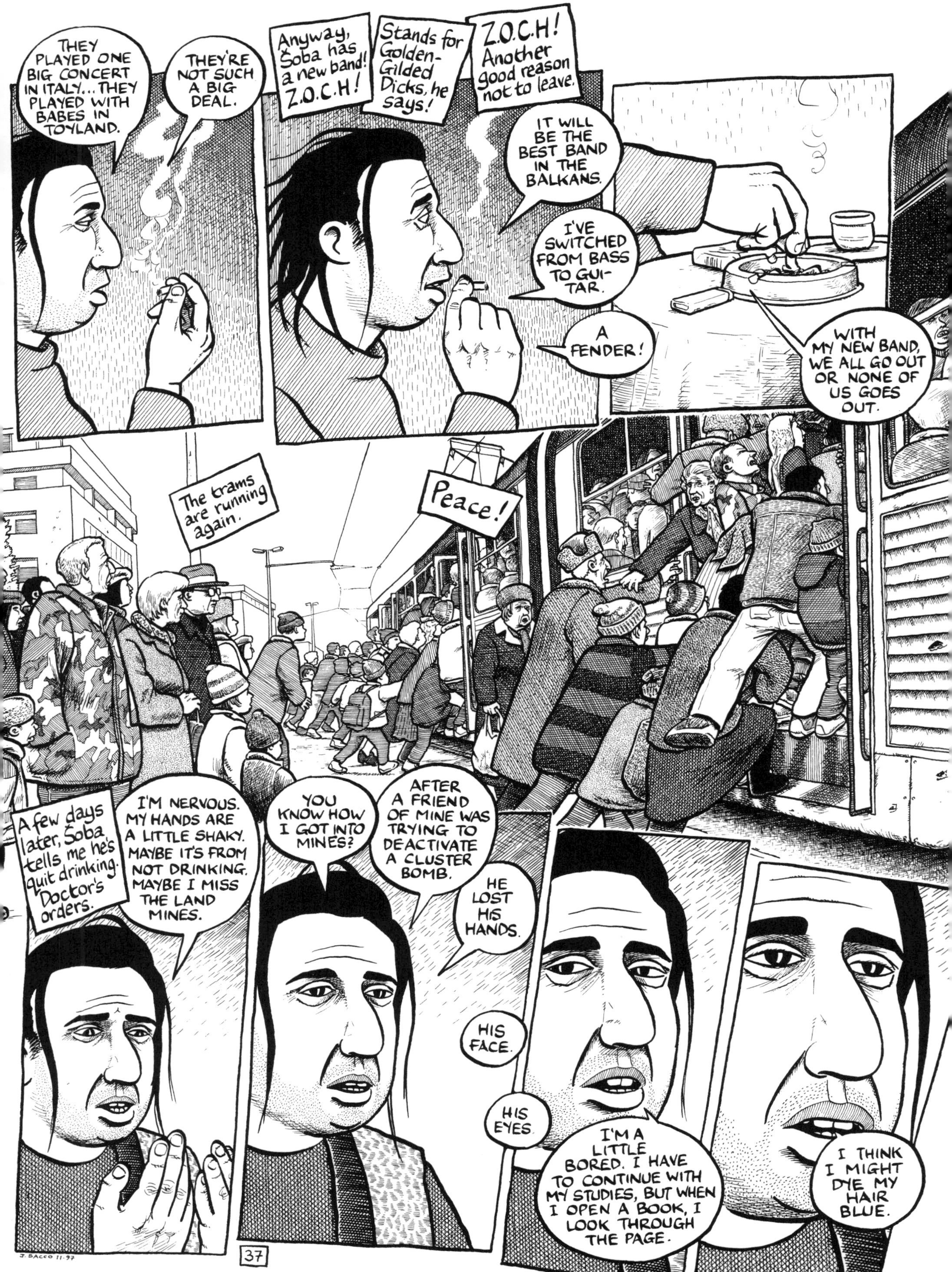

THEY PLAYED ONE BIG CONCERT IN ITALY... THEY PLAYED WITH BABES IN TOYLAND.
THEY'RE NOT SUCH A BIG DEAL.
Anyway, Šoba has a new band! Z.O.C.H!
Stands for Golden-Gilded Dicks, he says!
Z.O.C.H! Another good reason not to leave.
IT WILL BE THE BEST BAND IN THE BALKANS.
I'VE SWITCHED FROM BASS TO GUI-TAR.
A FENDER!
WITH MY NEW BAND, WE ALL GO OUT OR NONE OF US GOES OUT.
The trams are running again.
Peace!
A few days later, Šoba tells me he's quit drinking. Doctor's orders.
I'M NERVOUS. MY HANDS ARE A LITTLE SHAKY. MAYBE IT'S FROM NOT DRINKING. MAYBE I MISS THE LAND MINES.
YOU KNOW HOW I GOT INTO MINES?
AFTER A FRIEND OF MINE WAS TRYING TO DEACTIVATE A CLUSTER BOMB.
HE LOST HIS HANDS.
HIS FACE.
HIS EYES.
I'M A LITTLE BORED. I HAVE TO CONTINUE WITH MY STUDIES, BUT WHEN I OPEN A BOOK, I LOOK THROUGH THE PAGE.
I THINK I MIGHT DYE MY HAIR BLUE.
J. SACCO 11.97

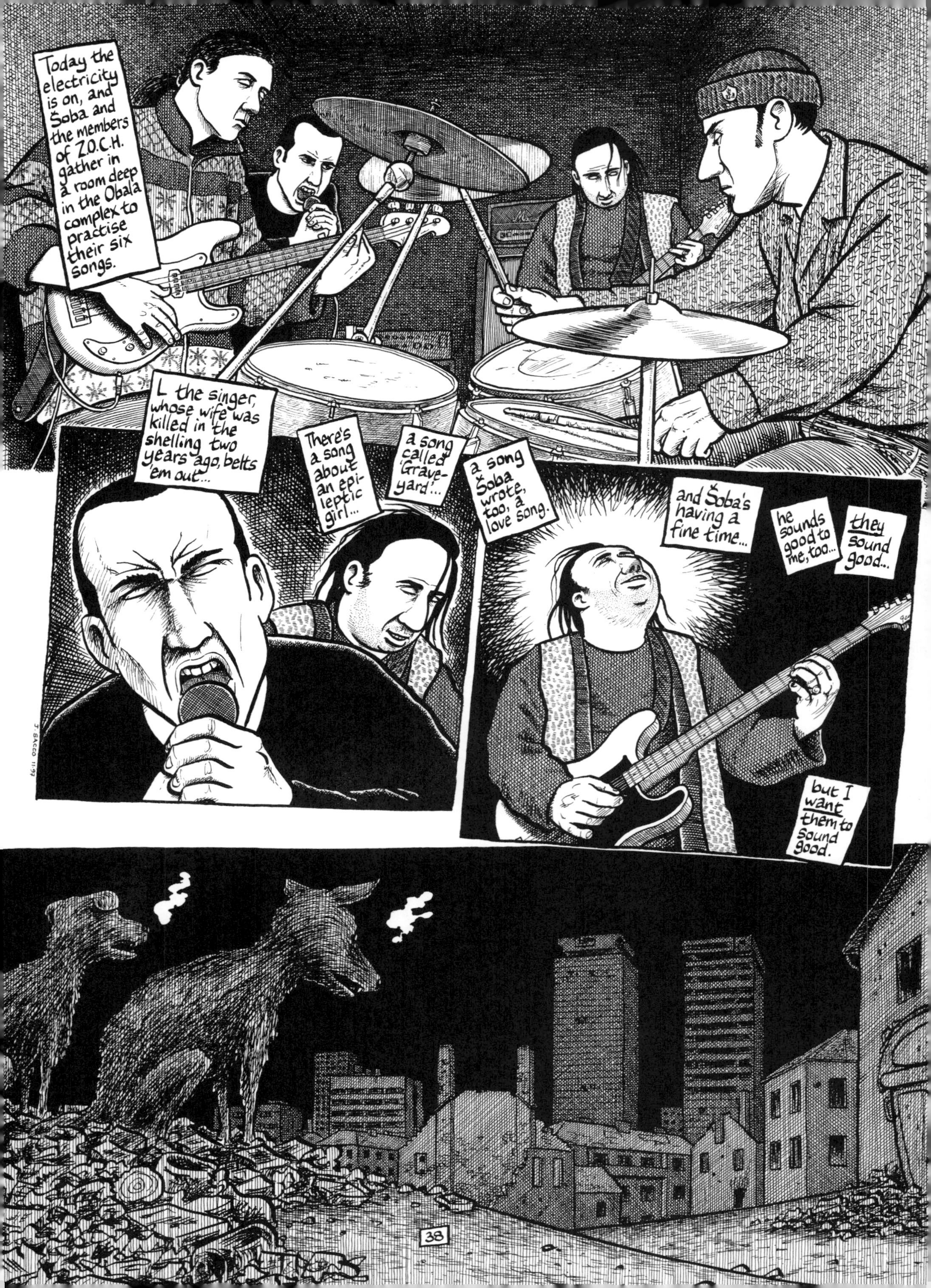
Today the electricity is on, and Šoba and the members of Z.O.C.H. gather in a room deep in the Obala complex to practise their six songs.
L the singer, whose wife was killed in the shelling two years ago, belts 'em out...
There's a song about an epileptic girl...
a song called 'Graveyard'...
a song Šoba wrote, too, a love song.
and Šoba's having a fine time...
he sounds good to me, too...
they sound good...
but I want them to sound good.
J. SACCO 11/97

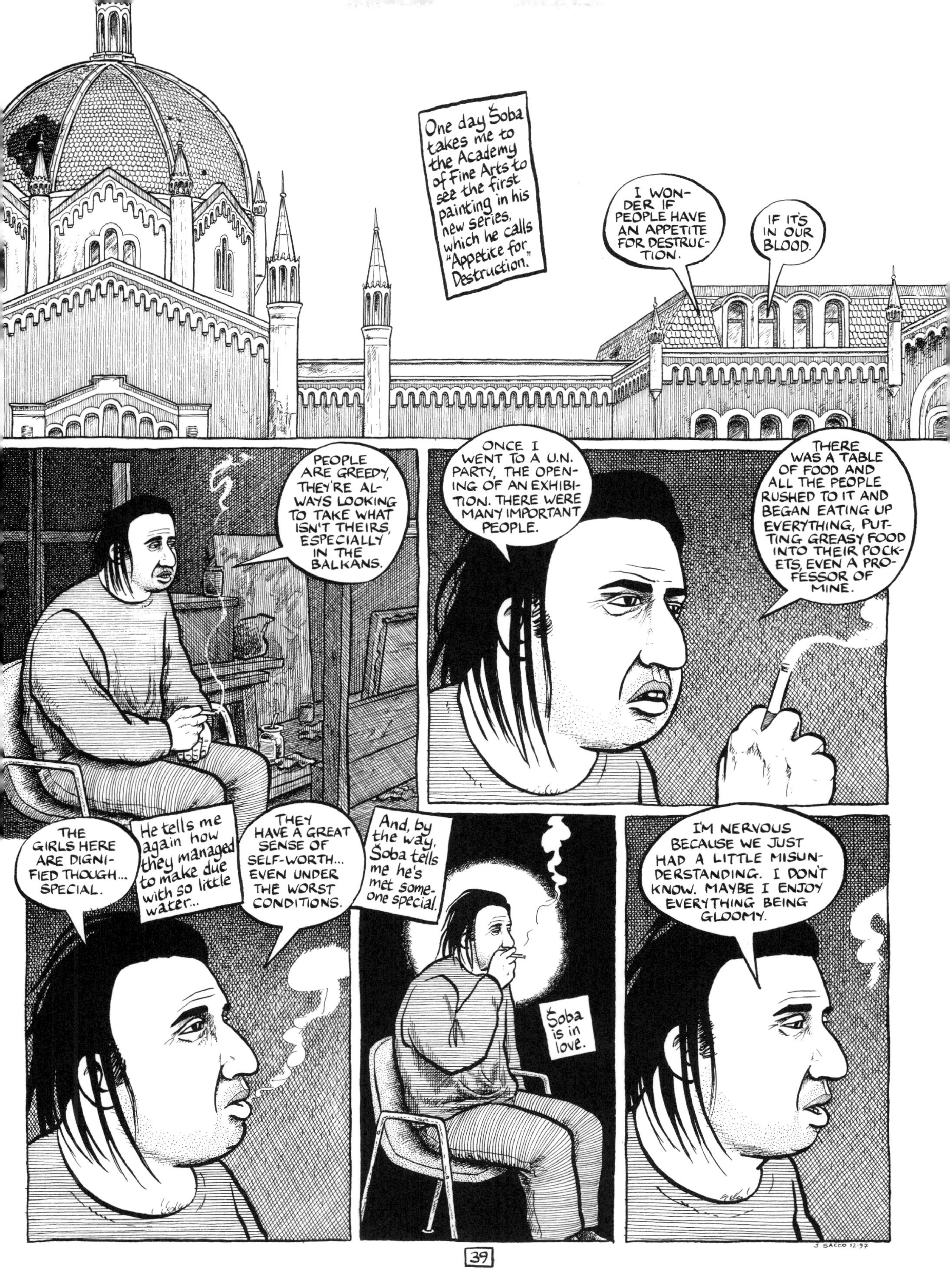
One day Šoba takes me to the Academy of Fine Arts to see the first painting in his new series, which he calls "Appetite for Destruction."
I WONDER IF PEOPLE HAVE AN APPETITE FOR DESTRUCTION.
IF IT'S IN OUR BLOOD.
PEOPLE ARE GREEDY, THEY'RE ALWAYS LOOKING TO TAKE WHAT ISN'T THEIRS, ESPECIALLY IN THE BALKANS.
ONCE I WENT TO A U.N. PARTY, THE OPENING OF AN EXHIBITION. THERE WERE MANY IMPORTANT PEOPLE.
THERE WAS A TABLE OF FOOD AND ALL THE PEOPLE RUSHED TO IT AND BEGAN EATING UP EVERYTHING, PUTTING GREASY FOOD INTO THEIR POCKETS, EVEN A PROFESSOR OF MINE.
THE GIRLS HERE ARE DIGNIFIED THOUGH... SPECIAL.
He tells me again how they managed to make due with so little water...
THEY HAVE A GREAT SENSE OF SELF-WORTH... EVEN UNDER THE WORST CONDITIONS.
And, by the way, Šoba tells me he's met someone special.
Šoba is in love.
I'M NERVOUS BECAUSE WE JUST HAD A LITTLE MISUNDERSTANDING. I DON'T KNOW. MAYBE I ENJOY EVERYTHING BEING GLOOMY.
J. SACCO 12·97

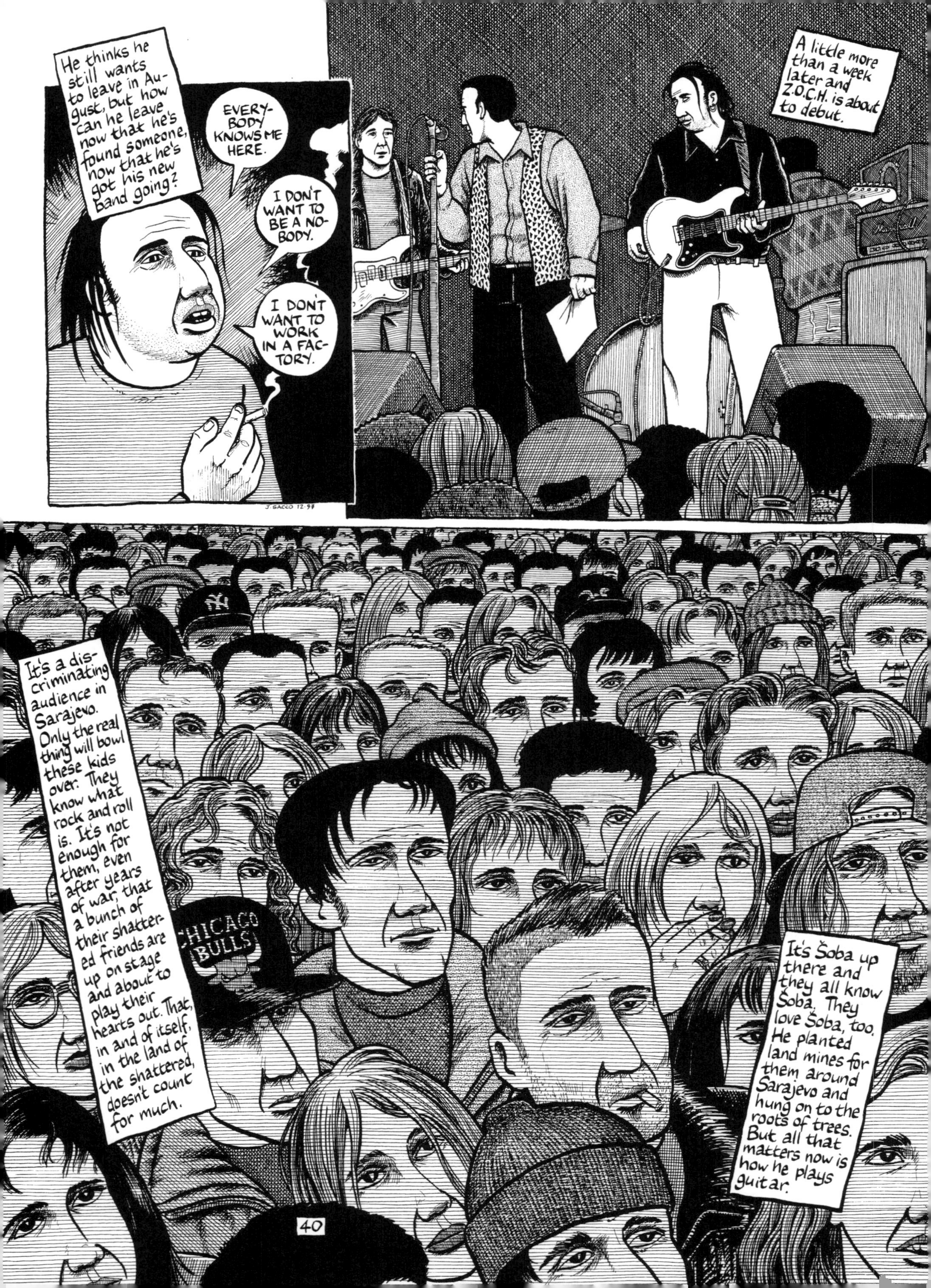
He thinks he still wants to leave in August, but how can he leave now that he's found someone, now that he's got his new band going?
EVERYBODY KNOWS ME HERE.
I DON'T WANT TO BE A NOBODY.
I DON'T WANT TO WORK IN A FACTORY.
J. SACCO 12·97
A little more than a week later and Z.O.C.H. is about to debut.
It's a discriminating audience in Sarajevo. Only the real thing will bowl these kids over. They know what rock and roll is. It's not enough for them, even after years of war, that a bunch of their shattered friends are up on stage and about to play their hearts out. That, in and of itself, in the land of the shattered, doesn't count for much.
CHICAGO BULLS
It's Šoba up there and they all know Šoba. They love Šoba, too. He planted land mines for them around Sarajevo and hung on to the roots of trees. But all that matters now is how he plays guitar.

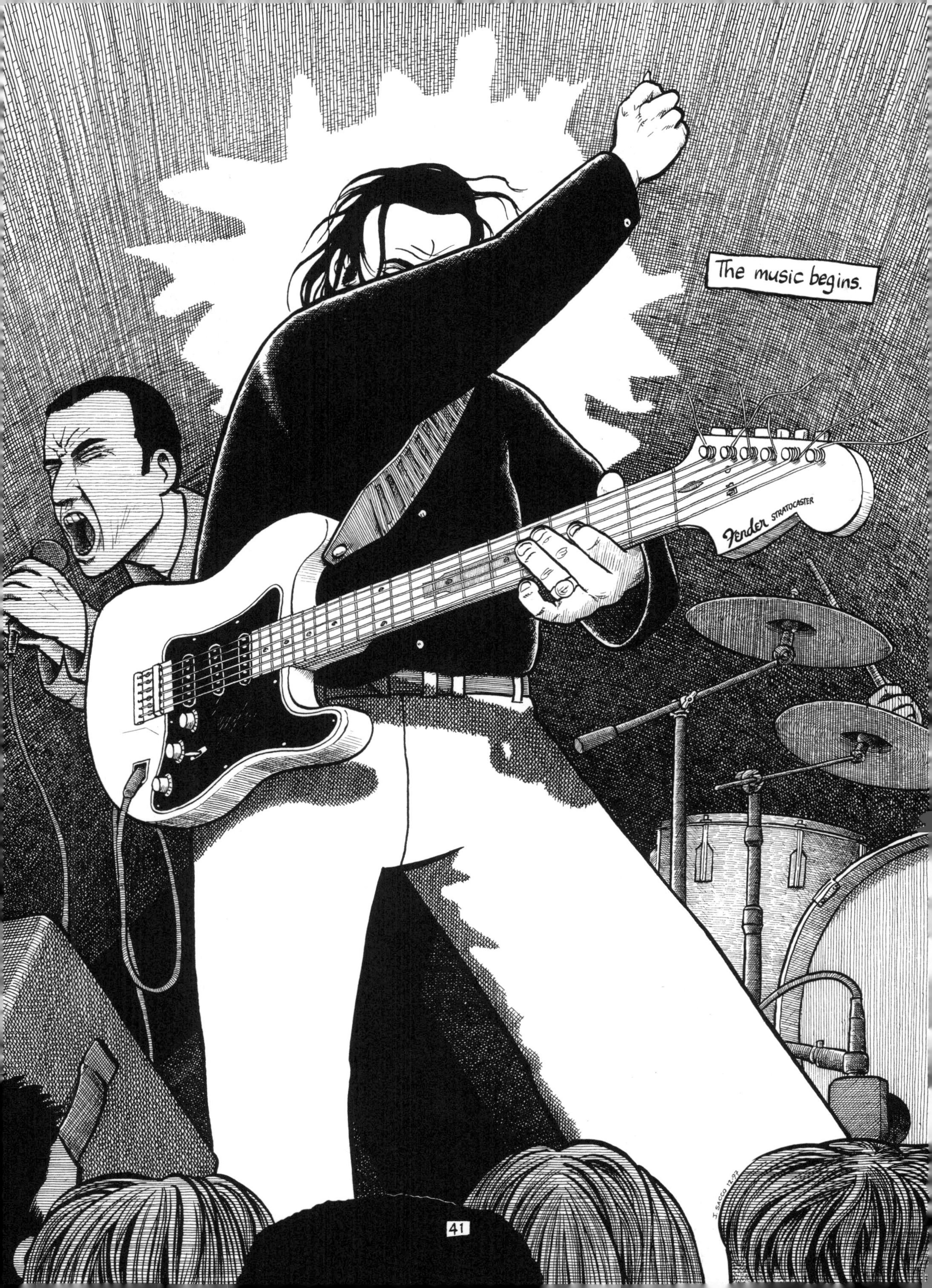
The music begins.
Fender STRATOCASTER

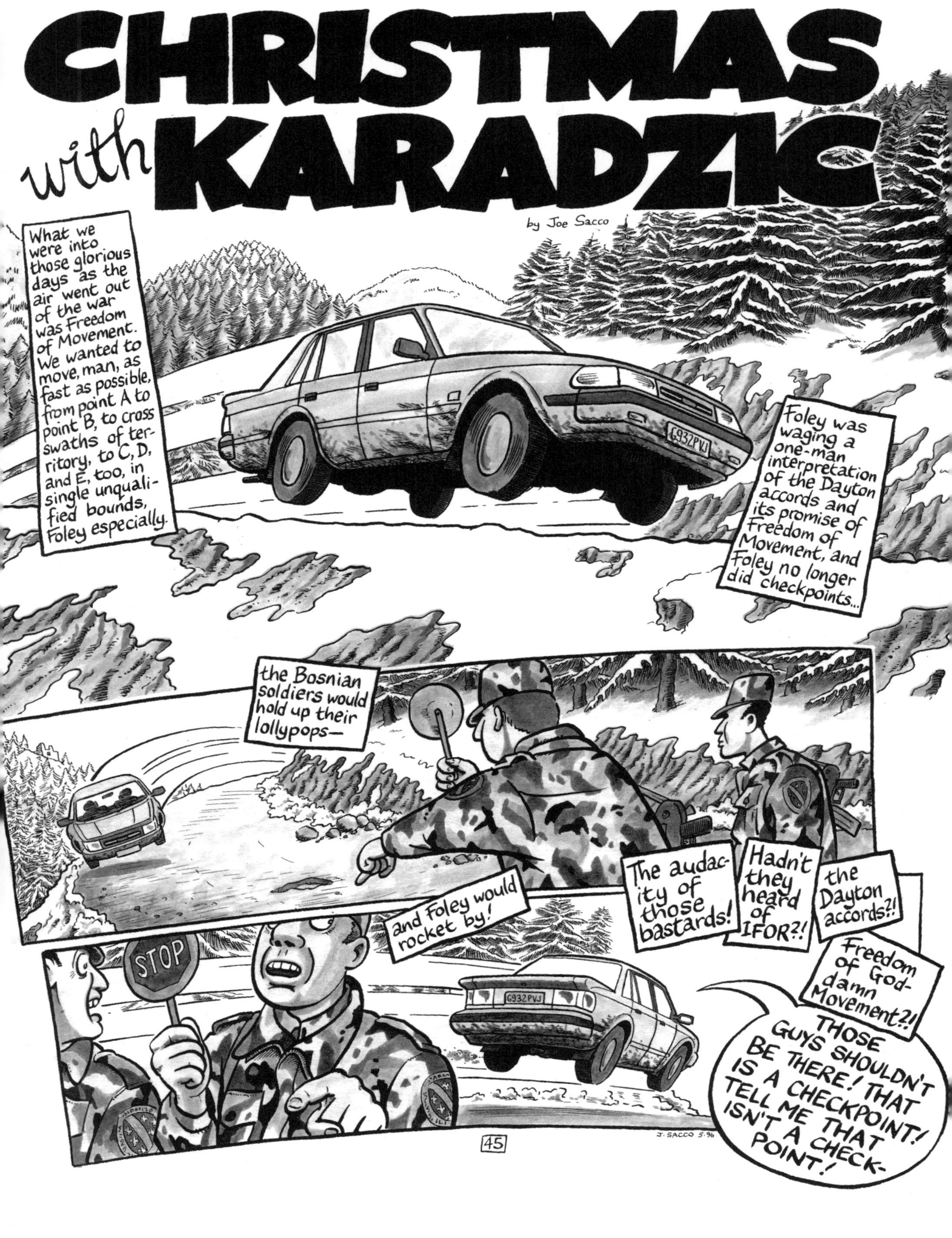
CHRISTMAS with KARADZIC
by Joe Sacco
What we were into those glorious days as the air went out of the war was Freedom of Movement. We wanted to move, man, as fast as possible, from point A to point B, to cross swaths of territory, to C, D, and E, too, in single unqualified bounds, Foley especially.
Foley was waging a one-man interpretation of the Dayton accords and its promise of Freedom of Movement, and Foley no longer did checkpoints...
G932PVJ
the Bosnian soldiers would hold up their lollypops—
and Foley would rocket by!
The audacity of those bastards!
Hadn't they heard of IFOR?!
the Dayton accords?!
Freedom of God-damn Movement?!
STOP
G932PVJ
THOSE GUYS SHOULDN'T BE THERE! THAT IS A CHECKPOINT! TELL ME THAT ISN'T A CHECK-POINT!
J. SACCO 5.96

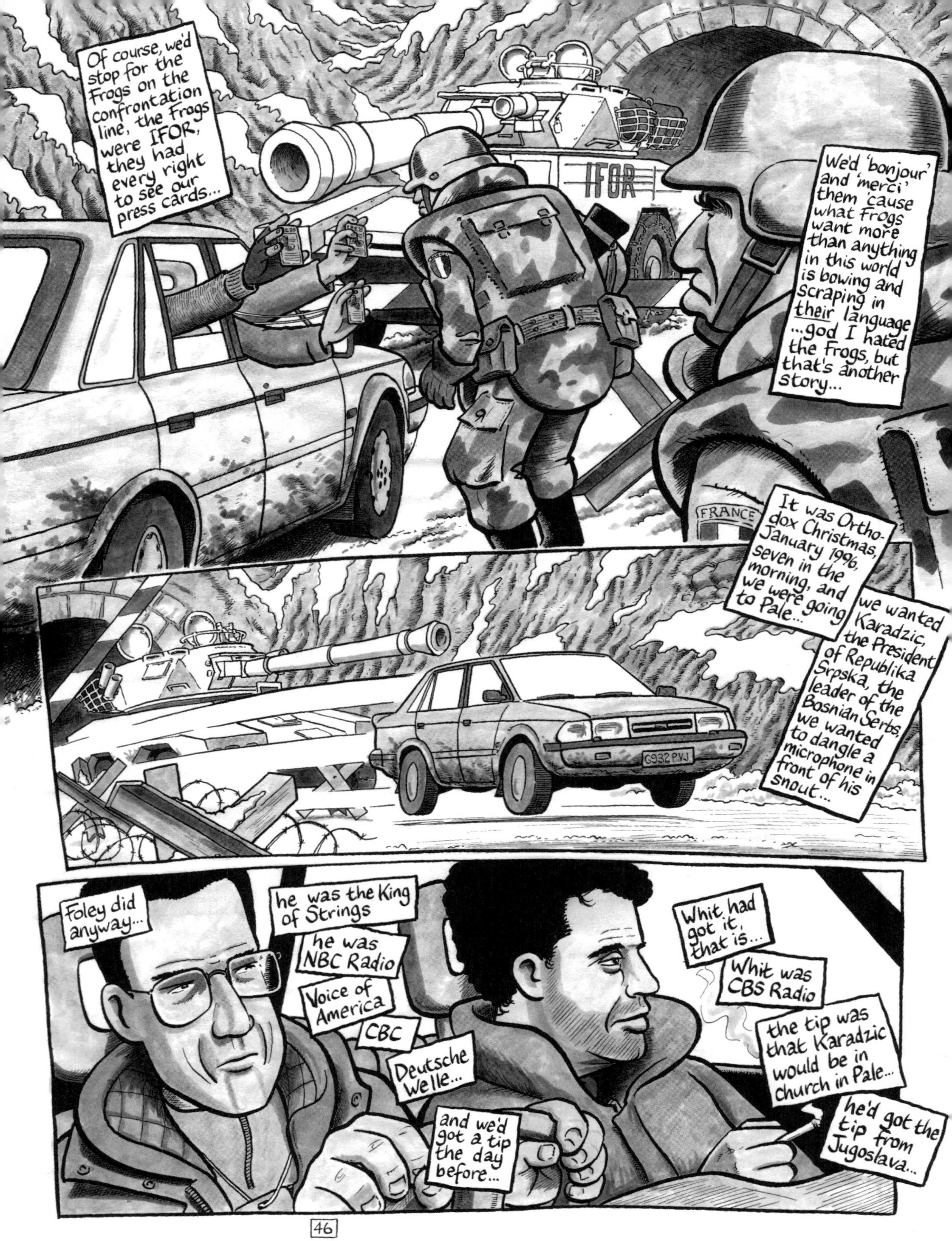
Of course, we'd stop for the Frogs on the confrontation line, the Frogs were IFOR, they had every right to see our press cards...
IFOR
We'd 'bonjour' and 'merci' them 'cause what Frogs want more than anything in this world is bowing and scraping in their language ...god I hated the Frogs, but that's another story...
FRANCE
It was Orthodox Christmas, January 1996, seven in the morning, and we were going to Pale...
we wanted Karadzic, the President of Republika Srpska, the leader of the Bosnian Serbs, we wanted to dangle a microphone in front of his snout...
G932 PVJ
Foley did anyway...
he was the King of Strings
he was NBC Radio
Voice of America
CBC
Deutsche Welle...
Whit had got it, that is...
Whit was CBS Radio
the tip was that Karadzic would be in church in Pale...
and we'd got a tip the day before...
he'd got the tip from Jugoslava...

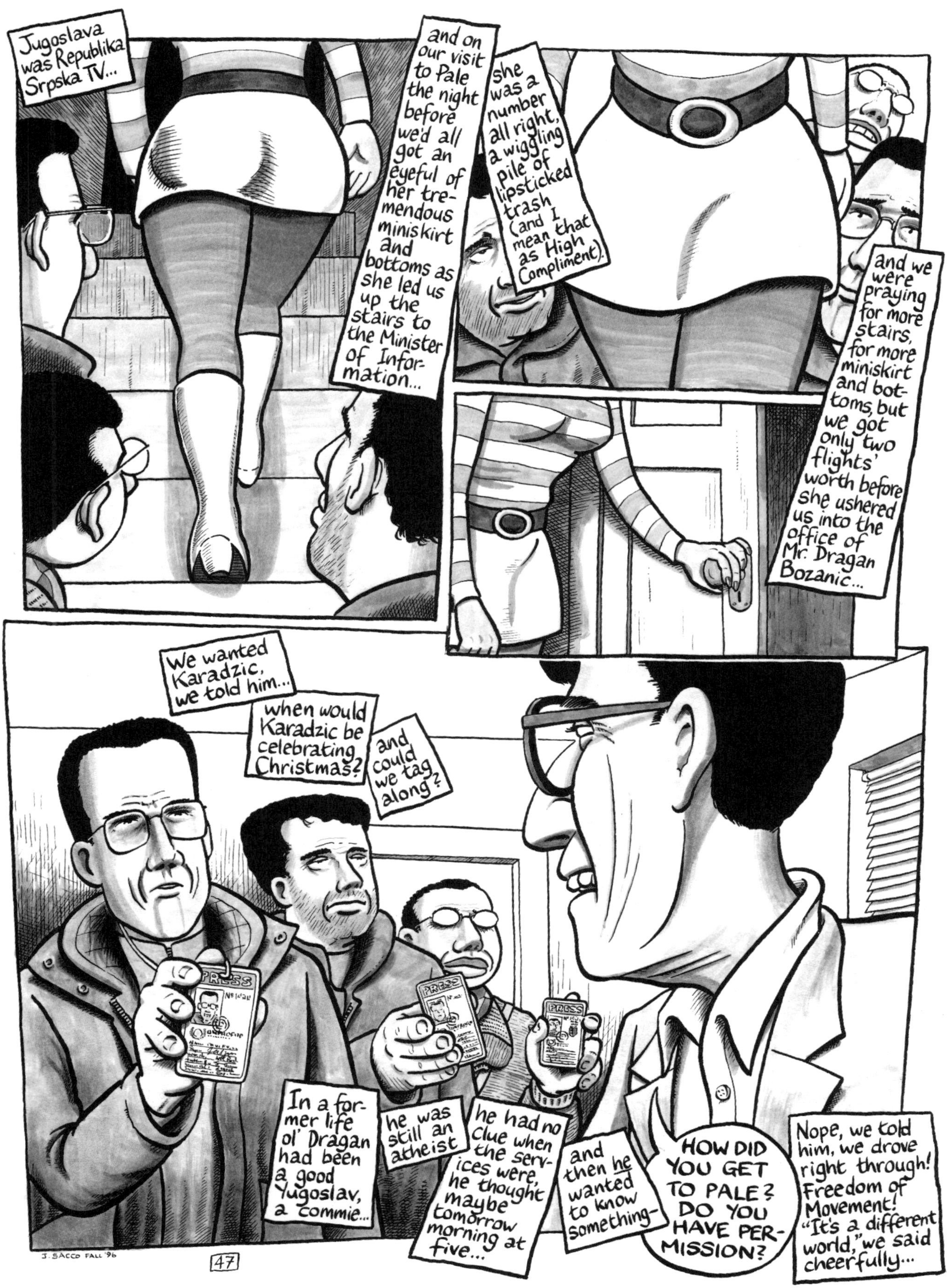
Jugoslava was Republika Srpska TV...
and on our visit to Pale the night before we'd all got an eyeful of her tremendous miniskirt and bottoms as she led us up the stairs to the Minister of Information...
she was a number all right, a wiggling pile of lipsticked trash (and I mean that as High Compliment).
and we were praying for more stairs, for more miniskirt and bottoms, but we got only two flights' worth before she ushered us into the office of Mr. Dragan Bozanic...
We wanted Karadzic, we told him...
when would Karadzic be celebrating Christmas?
and could we tag along?
PRESS
In a former life ol' Dragan had been a good Yugoslav, a commie...
he was still an atheist
he had no clue when the services were, he thought maybe tomorrow morning at five...
and then he wanted to know something-
HOW DID YOU GET TO PALE? DO YOU HAVE PERMISSION?
Nope, we told him, we drove right through! Freedom of Movement! "It's a different world," we said cheerfully...
J. SACCO FALL '96

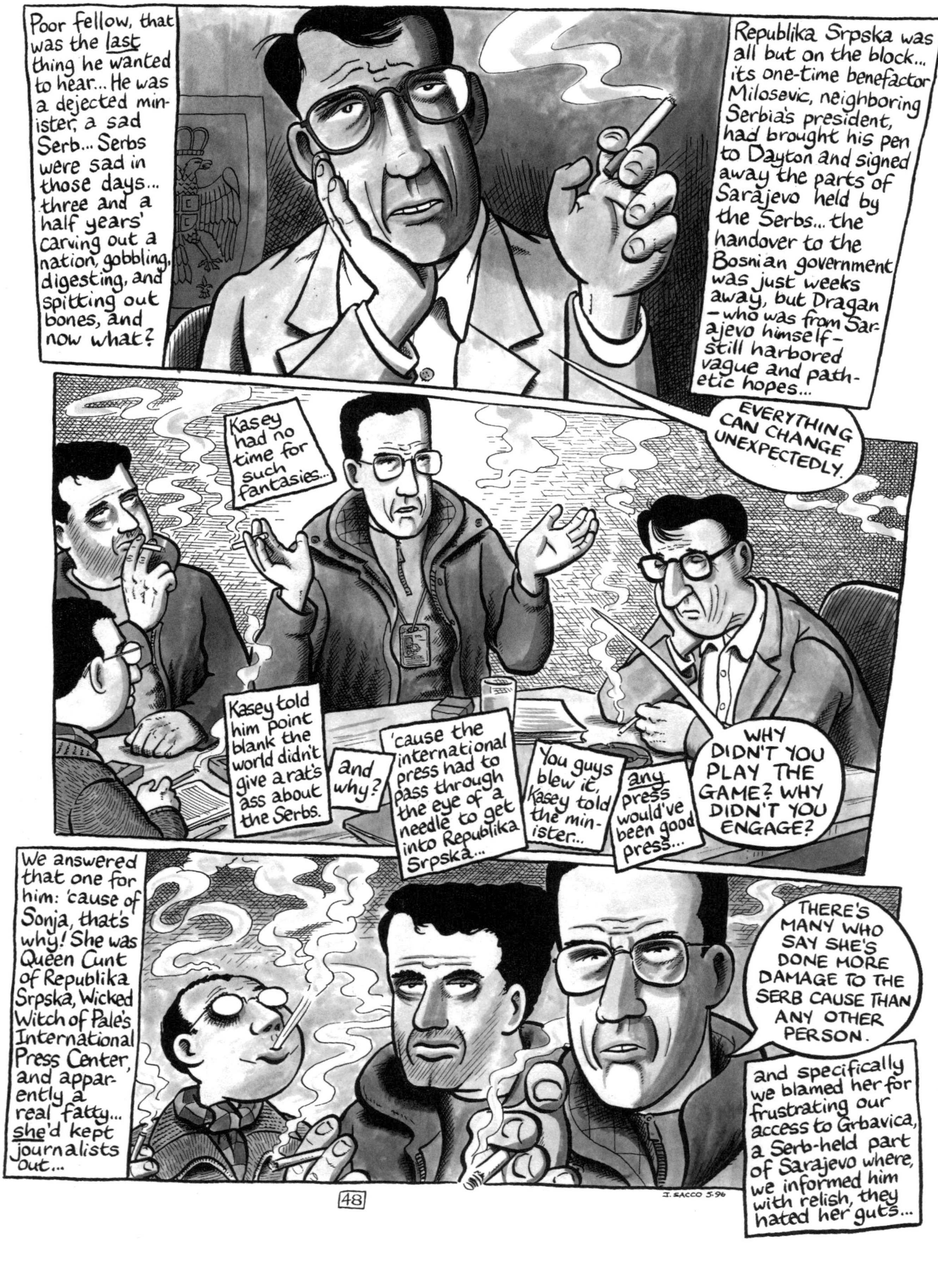
Poor fellow, that was the last thing he wanted to hear... He was a dejected minister, a sad Serb... Serbs were sad in those days... three and a half years' carving out a nation, gobbling, digesting, and spitting out bones, and now what?
Republika Srpska was all but on the block... its one-time benefactor Milosevic, neighboring Serbia's president, had brought his pen to Dayton and signed away the parts of Sarajevo held by the Serbs... the handover to the Bosnian government was just weeks away, but Dragan – who was from Sarajevo himself – still harbored vague and pathetic hopes...
EVERYTHING CAN CHANGE UNEXPECTEDLY.
Kasey had no time for such fantasies...
Kasey told him point blank the world didn't give a rat's ass about the Serbs.
and why?
'cause the international press had to pass through the eye of a needle to get into Republika Srpska...
You guys blew it, Kasey told the minister...
any press would've been good press...
WHY DIDN'T YOU PLAY THE GAME? WHY DIDN'T YOU ENGAGE?
We answered that one for him: 'cause of Sonja, that's why! She was Queen Cunt of Republika Srpska, Wicked Witch of Pale's International Press Center, and apparently a real fatty... she'd kept journalists out...
THERE'S MANY WHO SAY SHE'S DONE MORE DAMAGE TO THE SERB CAUSE THAN ANY OTHER PERSON.
and specifically we blamed her for frustrating our access to Grbavica, a Serb-held part of Sarajevo where, we informed him with relish, they hated her guts...
J. SACCO 5.96

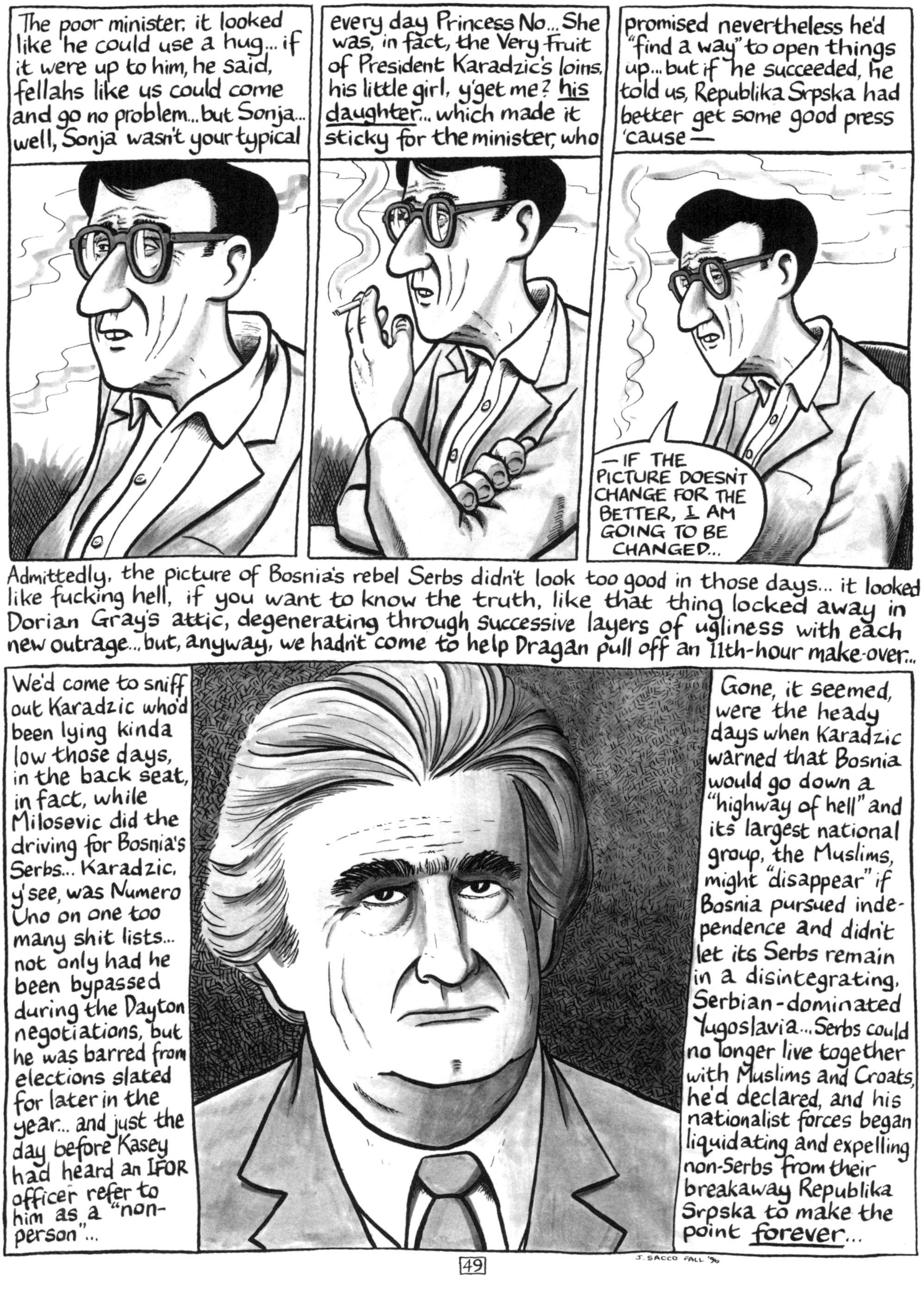
The poor minister, it looked like he could use a hug... if it were up to him, he said, fellahs like us could come and go no problem... but Sonja... well, Sonja wasn't your typical
every day Princess No... She was, in fact, the Very Fruit of President Karadzic's loins, his little girl, y'get me? his daughter... which made it sticky for the minister, who
promised nevertheless he'd "find a way" to open things up... but if he succeeded, he told us, Republika Srpska had better get some good press 'cause—
—IF THE PICTURE DOESN'T CHANGE FOR THE BETTER, I AM GOING TO BE CHANGED...
Admittedly, the picture of Bosnia's rebel Serbs didn't look too good in those days... it looked like fucking hell, if you want to know the truth, like that thing locked away in Dorian Gray's attic, degenerating through successive layers of ugliness with each new outrage... but, anyway, we hadn't come to help Dragan pull off an 11th-hour make-over...
We'd come to sniff out Karadzic who'd been lying kinda low those days, in the back seat, in fact, while Milosevic did the driving for Bosnia's Serbs... Karadzic, y'see, was Numero Uno on one too many shit lists... not only had he been bypassed during the Dayton negotiations, but he was barred from elections slated for later in the year... and just the day before Kasey had heard an IFOR officer refer to him as a "non-person"...
Gone, it seemed, were the heady days when Karadzic warned that Bosnia would go down a "highway of hell" and its largest national group, the Muslims, might "disappear" if Bosnia pursued independence and didn't let its Serbs remain in a disintegrating, Serbian-dominated Yugoslavia... Serbs could no longer live together with Muslims and Croats, he'd declared, and his nationalist forces began liquidating and expelling non-Serbs from their breakaway Republika Srpska to make the point forever...
J. SACCO FALL '96

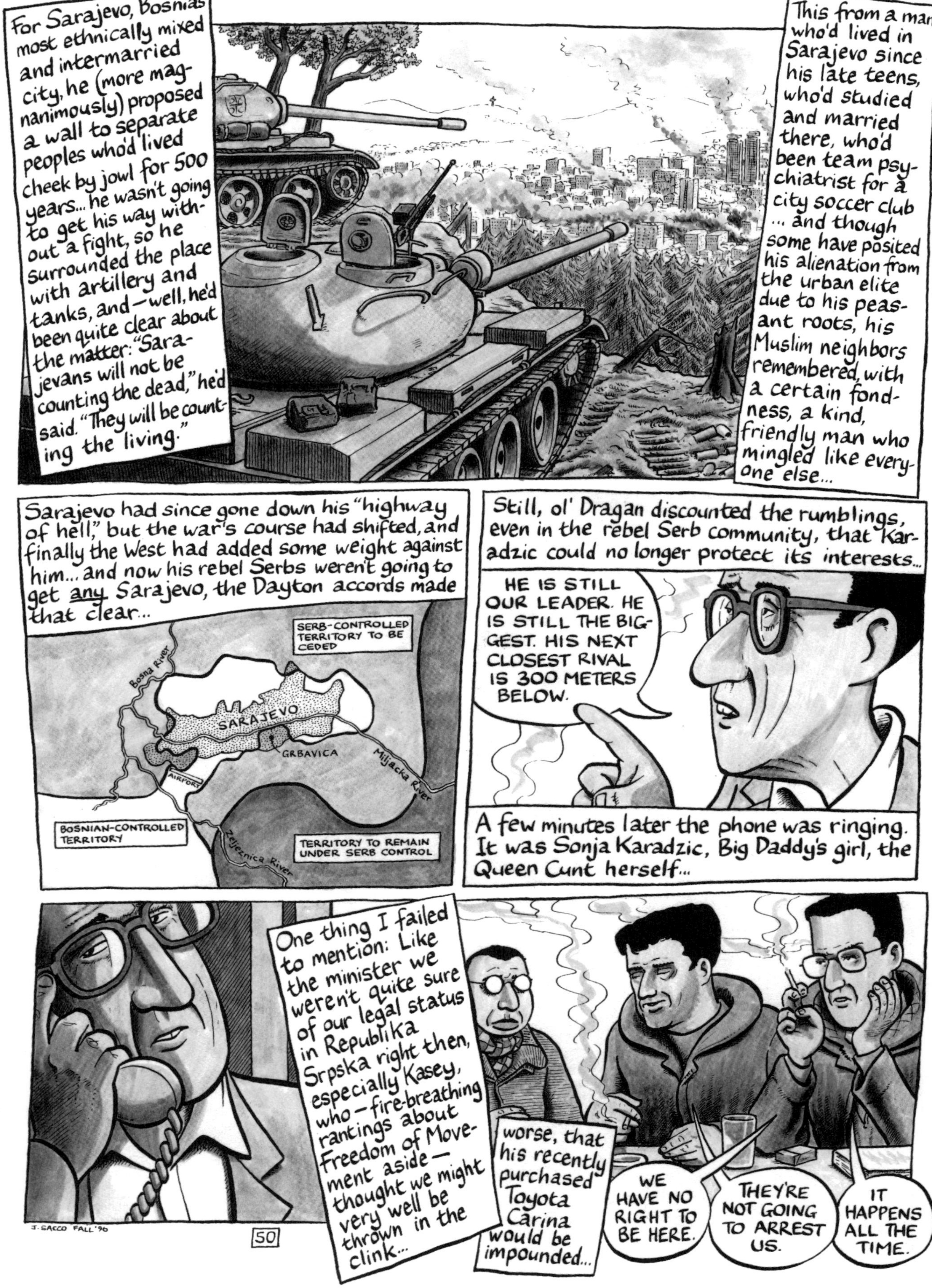
For Sarajevo, Bosnia's most ethnically mixed and intermarried city, he (more magnanimously) proposed a wall to separate peoples who'd lived cheek by jowl for 500 years... he wasn't going to get his way without a fight, so he surrounded the place with artillery and tanks, and—well, he'd been quite clear about the matter: "Sarajevans will not be counting the dead," he'd said. "They will be counting the living."
This from a man who'd lived in Sarajevo since his late teens, who'd studied and married there, who'd been team psychiatrist for a city soccer club ... and though some have posited his alienation from the urban elite due to his peasant roots, his Muslim neighbors remembered, with a certain fondness, a kind, friendly man who mingled like everyone else...
Sarajevo had since gone down his "highway of hell," but the war's course had shifted, and finally the West had added some weight against him... and now his rebel Serbs weren't going to get any Sarajevo, the Dayton accords made that clear...
SERB-CONTROLLED TERRITORY TO BE CEDED
Bosna River
SARAJEVO
GRBAVICA
Miljacka River
AIRPORT
BOSNIAN-CONTROLLED TERRITORY
Zeljeznica River
TERRITORY TO REMAIN UNDER SERB CONTROL
Still, ol' Dragan discounted the rumblings, even in the rebel Serb community, that Karadzic could no longer protect its interests...
HE IS STILL OUR LEADER. HE IS STILL THE BIGGEST. HIS NEXT CLOSEST RIVAL IS 300 METERS BELOW.
A few minutes later the phone was ringing. It was Sonja Karadzic, Big Daddy's girl, the Queen Cunt herself...
One thing I failed to mention: Like the minister we weren't quite sure of our legal status in Republika Srpska right then, especially Kasey, who—fire-breathing rantings about Freedom of Movement aside—thought we might very well be thrown in the clink...
worse, that his recently purchased Toyota Carina would be impounded...
WE HAVE NO RIGHT TO BE HERE.
THEY'RE NOT GOING TO ARREST US.
IT HAPPENS ALL THE TIME.
J. SACCO FALL '96

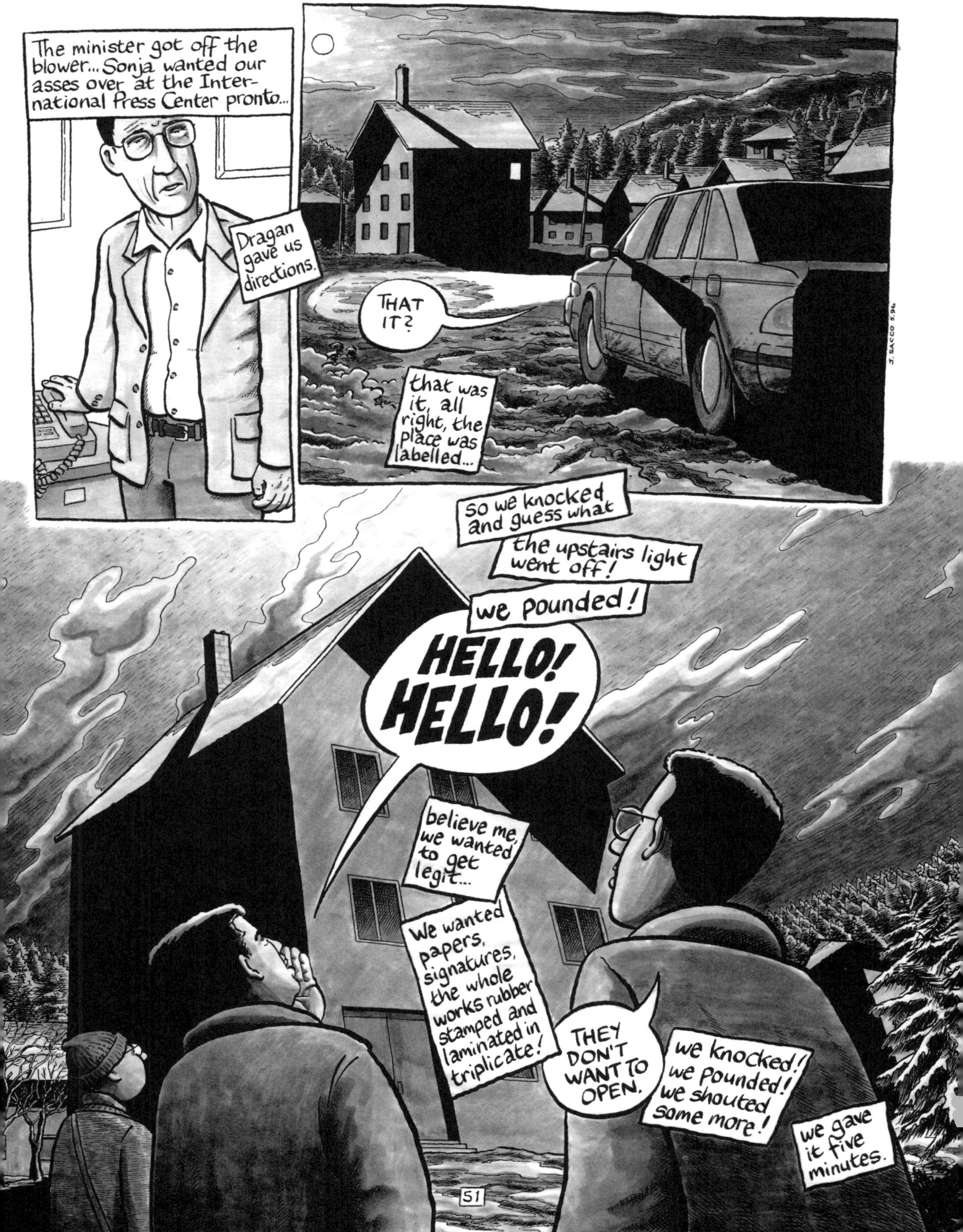
The minister got off the blower... Sonja wanted our asses over at the International Press Center pronto...
Dragan gave us directions.
THAT IT?
that was it, all right, the place was labelled...
J. SACCO 5.96
so we knocked and guess what
the upstairs light went off!
we pounded!
HELLO! HELLO!
believe me, we wanted to get legit...
We wanted papers, signatures, the whole works rubber stamped and laminated in triplicate!
THEY DON'T WANT TO OPEN.
we knocked! we pounded! we shouted some more!
we gave it five minutes.

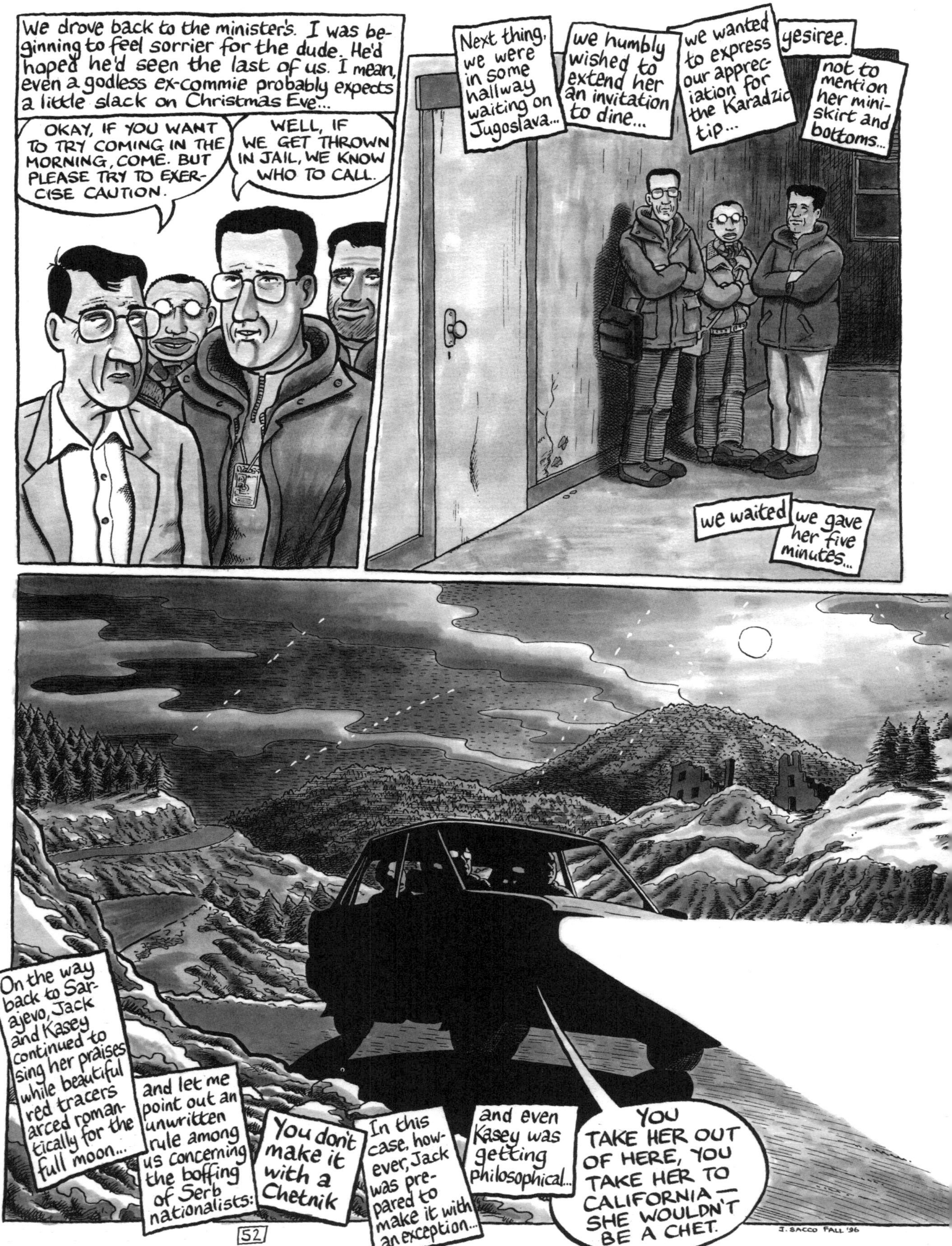
We drove back to the minister's. I was beginning to feel sorrier for the dude. He'd hoped he'd seen the last of us. I mean, even a godless ex-commie probably expects a little slack on Christmas Eve...
OKAY, IF YOU WANT TO TRY COMING IN THE MORNING, COME. BUT PLEASE TRY TO EXERCISE CAUTION.
WELL, IF WE GET THROWN IN JAIL, WE KNOW WHO TO CALL.
Next thing, we were in some hallway waiting on Jugoslava...
we humbly wished to extend her an invitation to dine...
we wanted to express our appreciation for the Karadzic tip...
yesiree.
not to mention her miniskirt and bottoms...
we waited
we gave her five minutes...
On the way back to Sarajevo, Jack and Kasey continued to sing her praises while beautiful red tracers arced romantically for the full moon...
and let me point out an unwritten rule among us concerning the boffing of Serb nationalists:
You don't make it with a Chetnik
In this case, however, Jack was prepared to make it with an exception...
and even Kasey was getting philosophical...
YOU TAKE HER OUT OF HERE, YOU TAKE HER TO CALIFORNIA — SHE WOULDN'T BE A CHET.
J. SACCO FALL '96

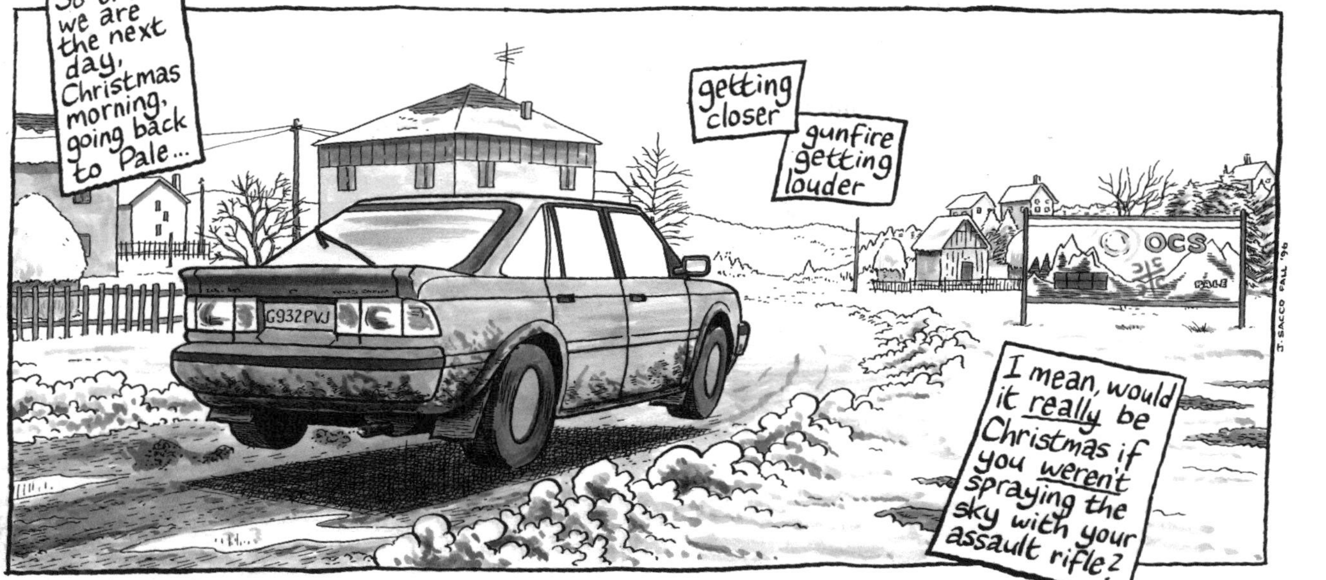
So there we are the next day, Christmas morning, going back to Pale...
getting closer
gunfire getting louder
G932PVJ
OCS
I mean, would it really be Christmas if you weren't spraying the sky with your assault rifle?

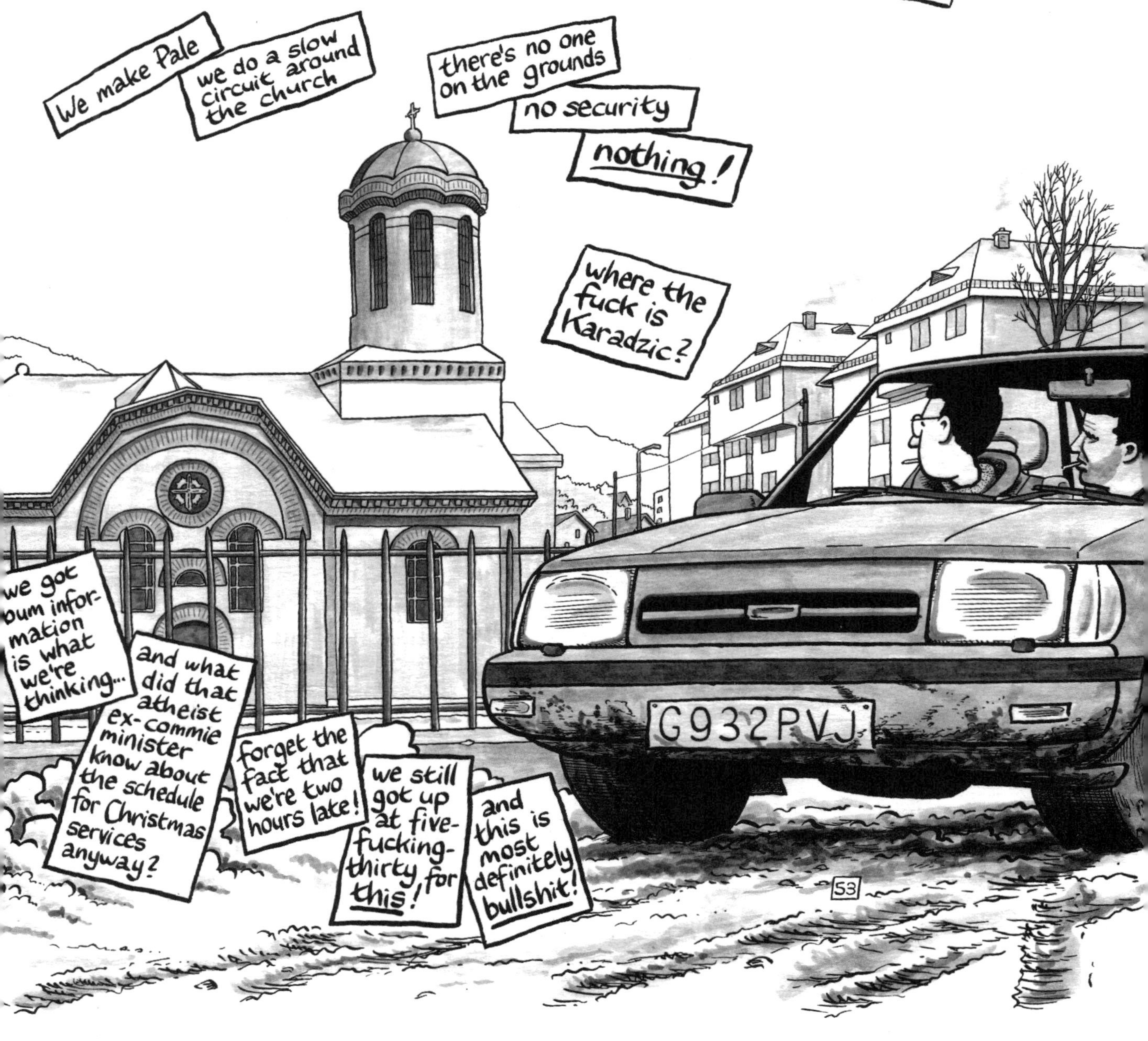
We make Pale
we do a slow circuit around the church
there's no one on the grounds
no security
nothing!
where the fuck is Karadzic?
we got bum information is what we're thinking...
and what did that atheist ex-commie minister know about the schedule for Christmas services anyway?
forget the fact that we're two hours late!
we still got up at five-fucking-thirty for this!
and this is most definitely bullshit!
G932PVJ

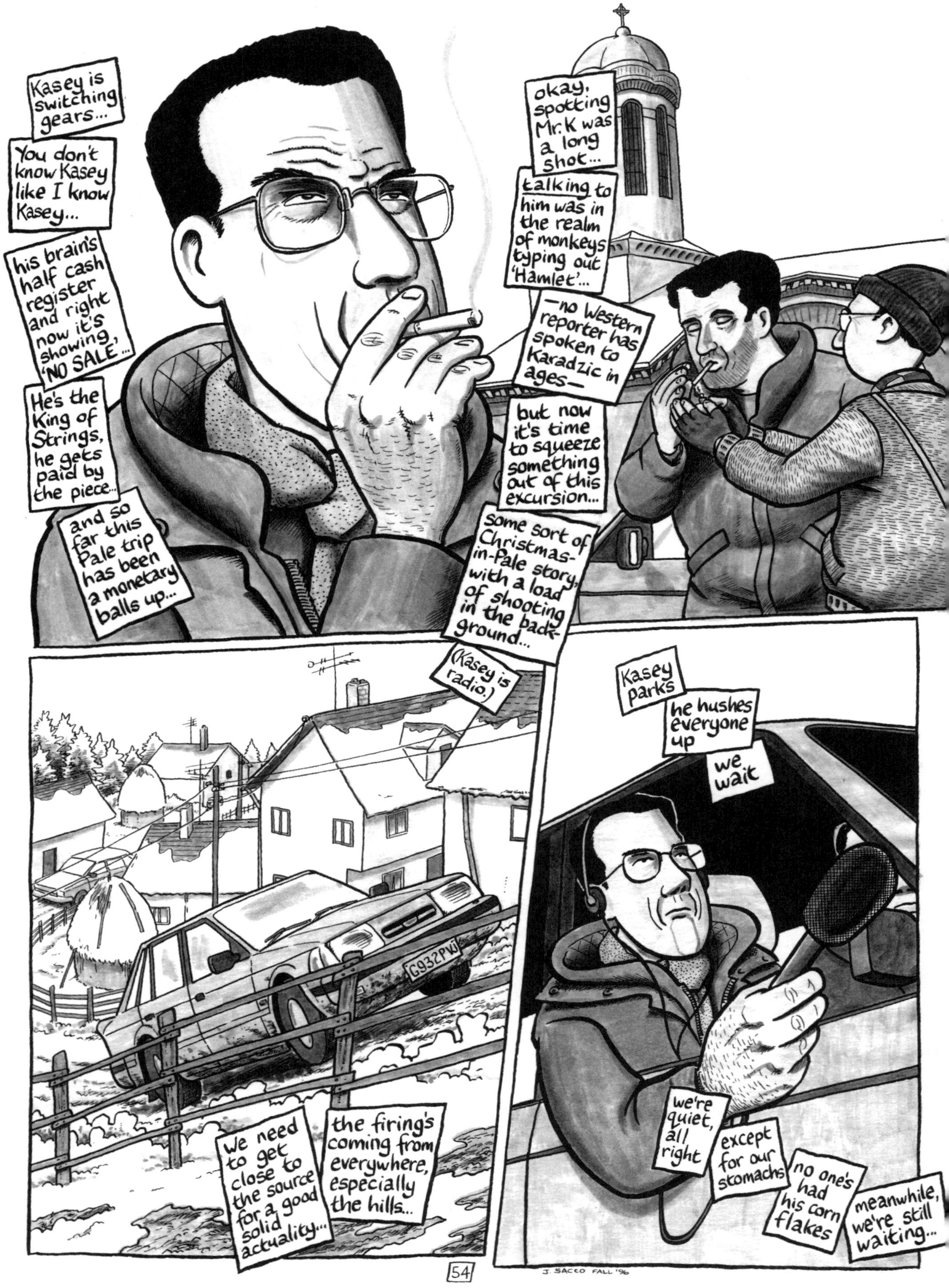
Kasey is switching gears...
You don't know Kasey like I know Kasey...
his brain's half cash register and right now it's showing, 'NO SALE'...
He's the King of Strings, he gets paid by the piece...
and so far this Pale trip has been a monetary balls up...
okay, spotting Mr. K was a long shot...
talking to him was in the realm of monkeys typing out 'Hamlet'...
—no Western reporter has spoken to Karadzic in ages—
but now it's time to squeeze something out of this excursion...
some sort of Christmas-in-Pale story, with a load of shooting in the background...
(Kasey is radio.)
G932PVJ
We need to get close to the source for a good solid actuality...
the firing's coming from everywhere, especially the hills...
Kasey parks
he hushes everyone up
we wait
we're quiet, all right
except for our stomachs
no one's had his corn flakes
meanwhile, we're still waiting...
J. SACCO FALL '96

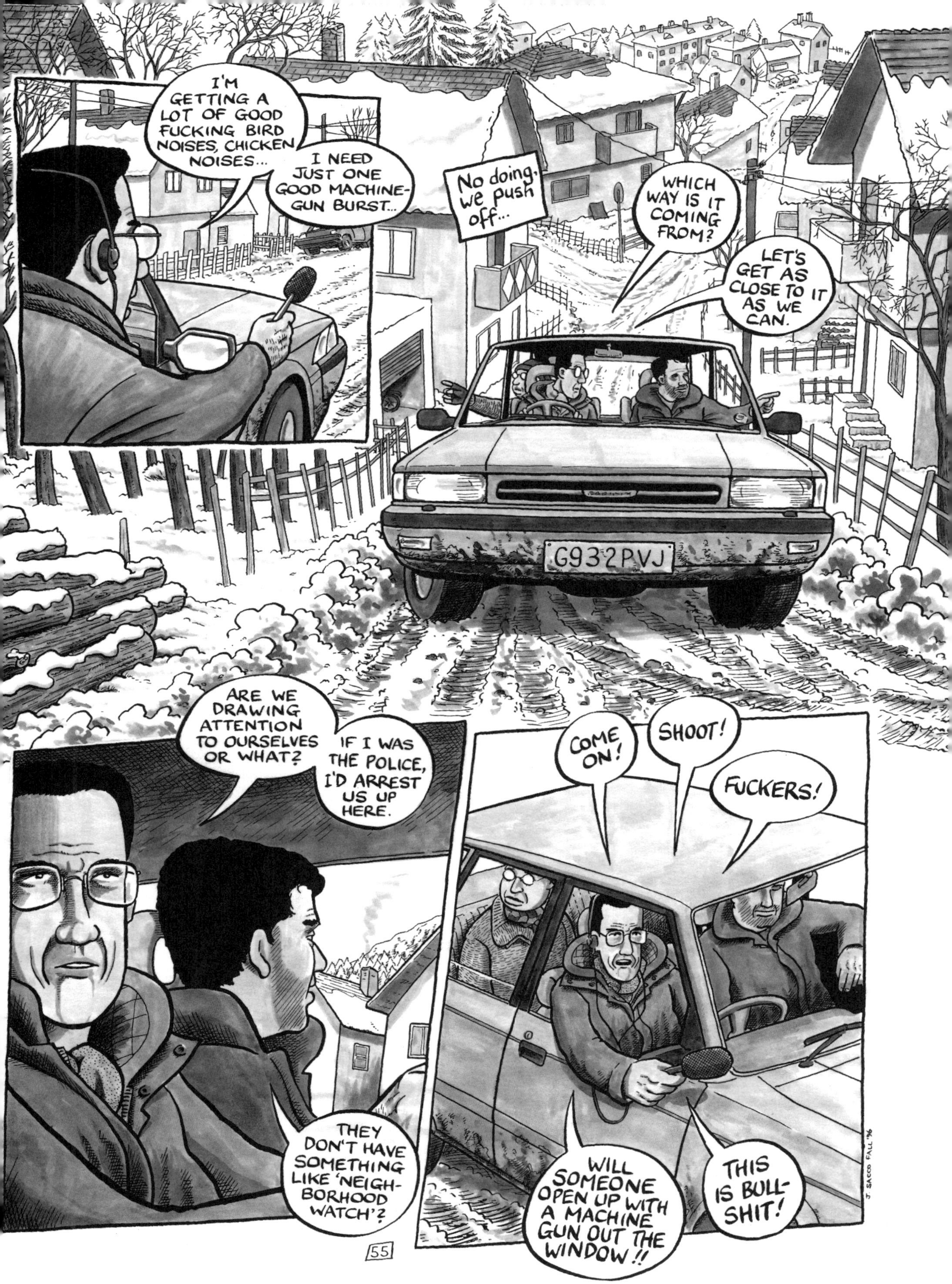

I'M GETTING A LOT OF GOOD FUCKING BIRD NOISES, CHICKEN NOISES...
I NEED JUST ONE GOOD MACHINE-GUN BURST...
No doing, we push off...
WHICH WAY IS IT COMING FROM?
LET'S GET AS CLOSE TO IT AS WE CAN.
G932PVJ
ARE WE DRAWING ATTENTION TO OURSELVES OR WHAT?
IF I WAS THE POLICE, I'D ARREST US UP HERE.
THEY DON'T HAVE SOMETHING LIKE 'NEIGHBORHOOD WATCH'?
COME ON!
SHOOT!
FUCKERS!
WILL SOMEONE OPEN UP WITH A MACHINE GUN OUT THE WINDOW!!
THIS IS BULLSHIT!
J. SACCO FALL '96

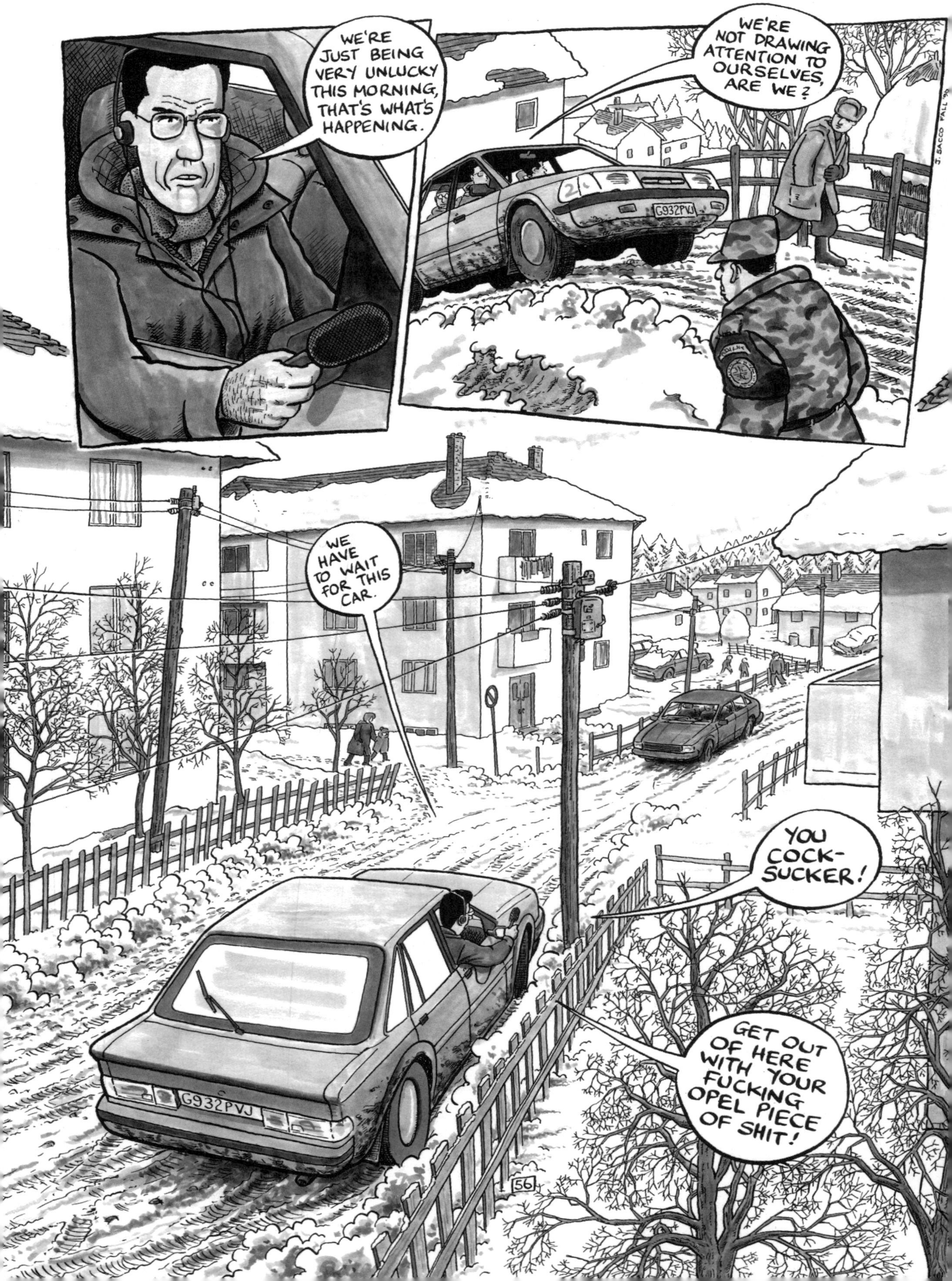
WE'RE JUST BEING VERY UNLUCKY THIS MORNING, THAT'S WHAT'S HAPPENING.
WE'RE NOT DRAWING ATTENTION TO OURSELVES, ARE WE?
J. SACCO FALL '96
G932PVJ
WE HAVE TO WAIT FOR THIS CAR.
YOU COCK-SUCKER!
GET OUT OF HERE WITH YOUR FUCKING OPEL PIECE OF SHIT!
G932PVJ

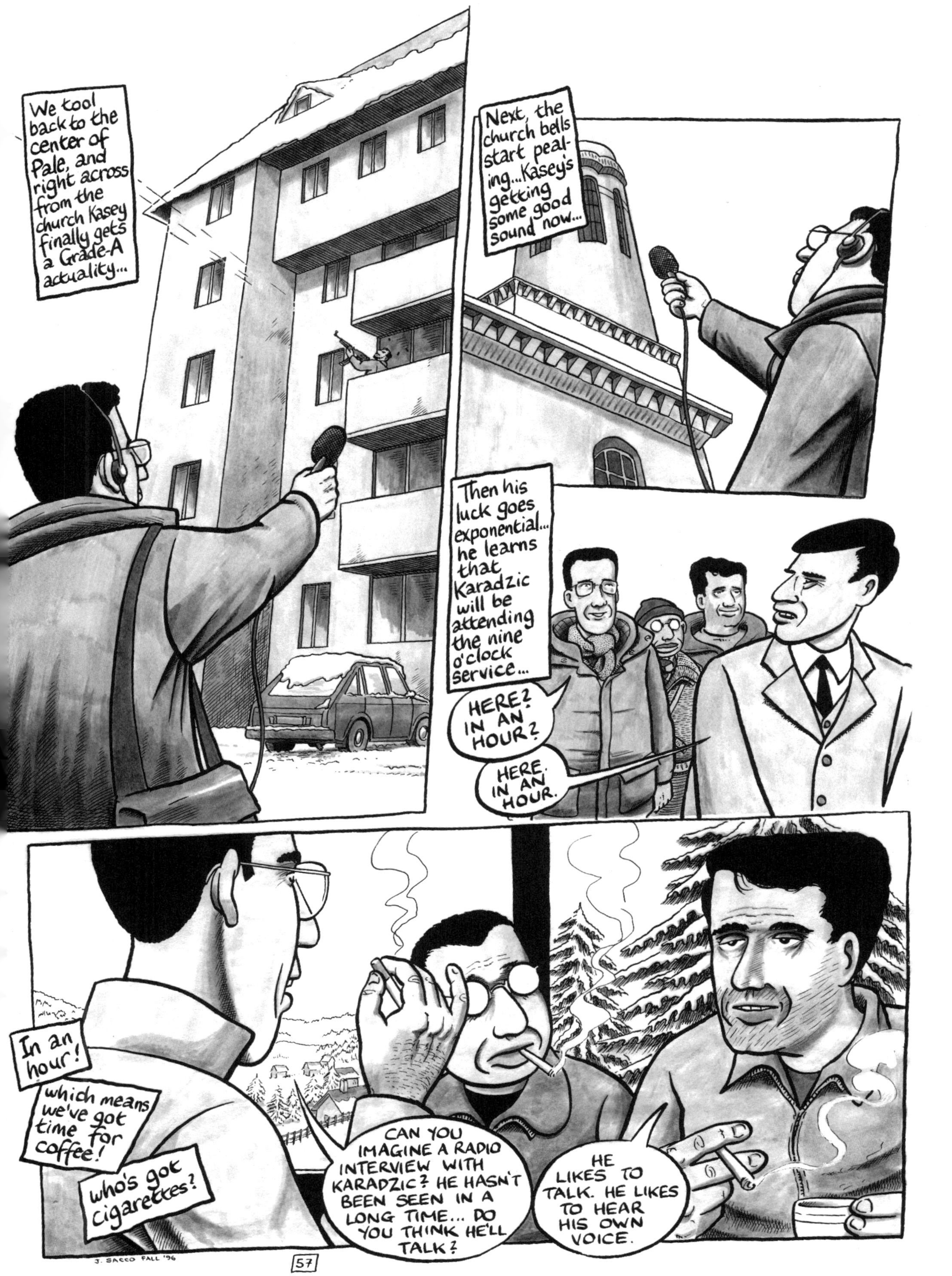
We tool back to the center of Pale, and right across from the church Kasey finally gets a Grade-A actuality...
Next, the church bells start pealing...Kasey's getting some good sound now...
Then his luck goes exponential... he learns that Karadzic will be attending the nine o'clock service...
HERE? IN AN HOUR?
HERE. IN AN HOUR.
In an hour!
which means we've got time for coffee!
who's got cigarettes?
CAN YOU IMAGINE A RADIO INTERVIEW WITH KARADZIC? HE HASN'T BEEN SEEN IN A LONG TIME... DO YOU THINK HE'LL TALK?
HE LIKES TO TALK. HE LIKES TO HEAR HIS OWN VOICE.
J. SACCO FALL '96

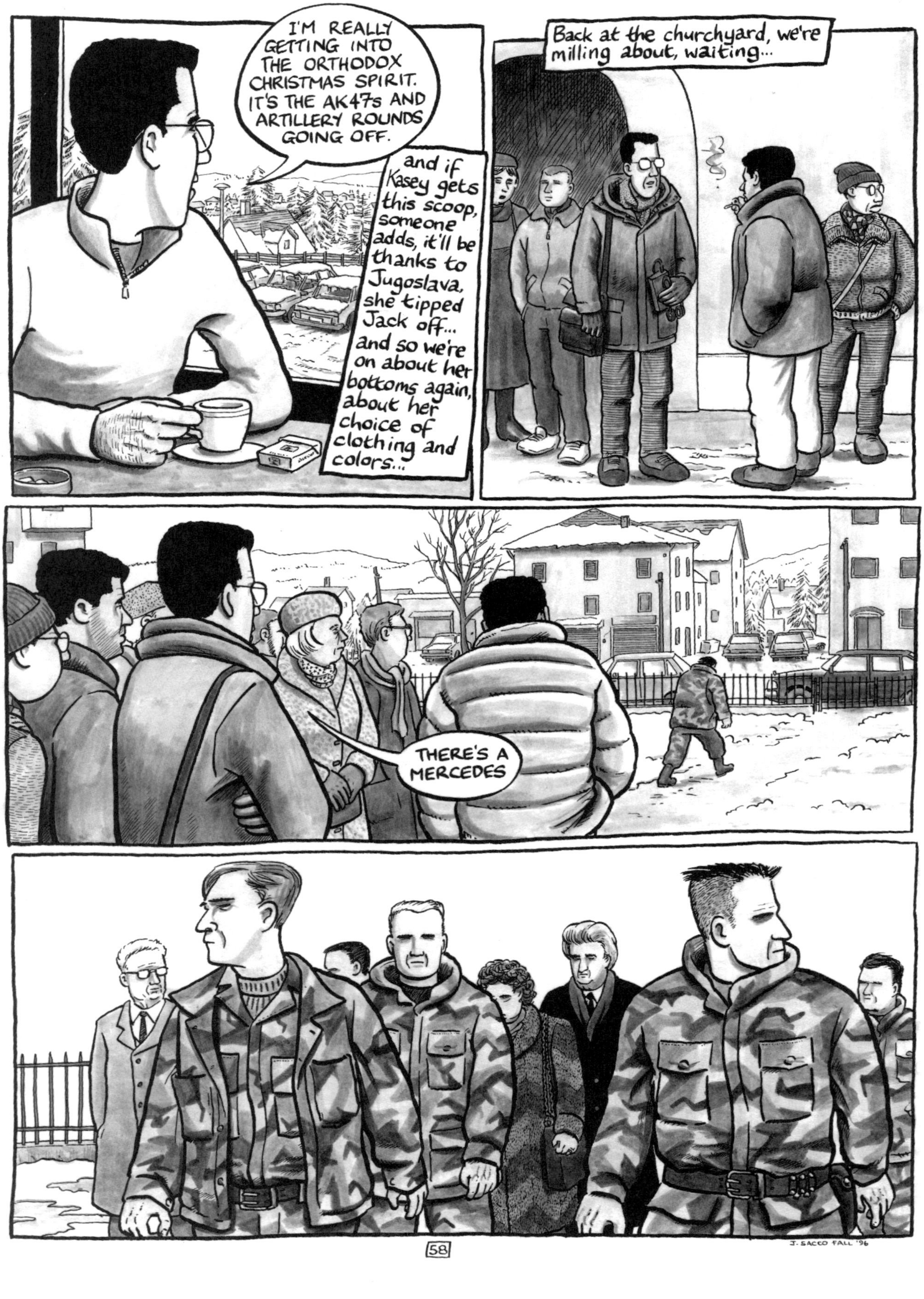

I'M REALLY GETTING INTO THE ORTHODOX CHRISTMAS SPIRIT. IT'S THE AK47s AND ARTILLERY ROUNDS GOING OFF.
and if Kasey gets this scoop, someone adds, it'll be thanks to Jugoslava, she tipped Jack off... and so we're on about her bottoms again, about her choice of clothing and colors...
Back at the churchyard, we're milling about, waiting...
THERE'S A MERCEDES
J. SACCO FALL '96

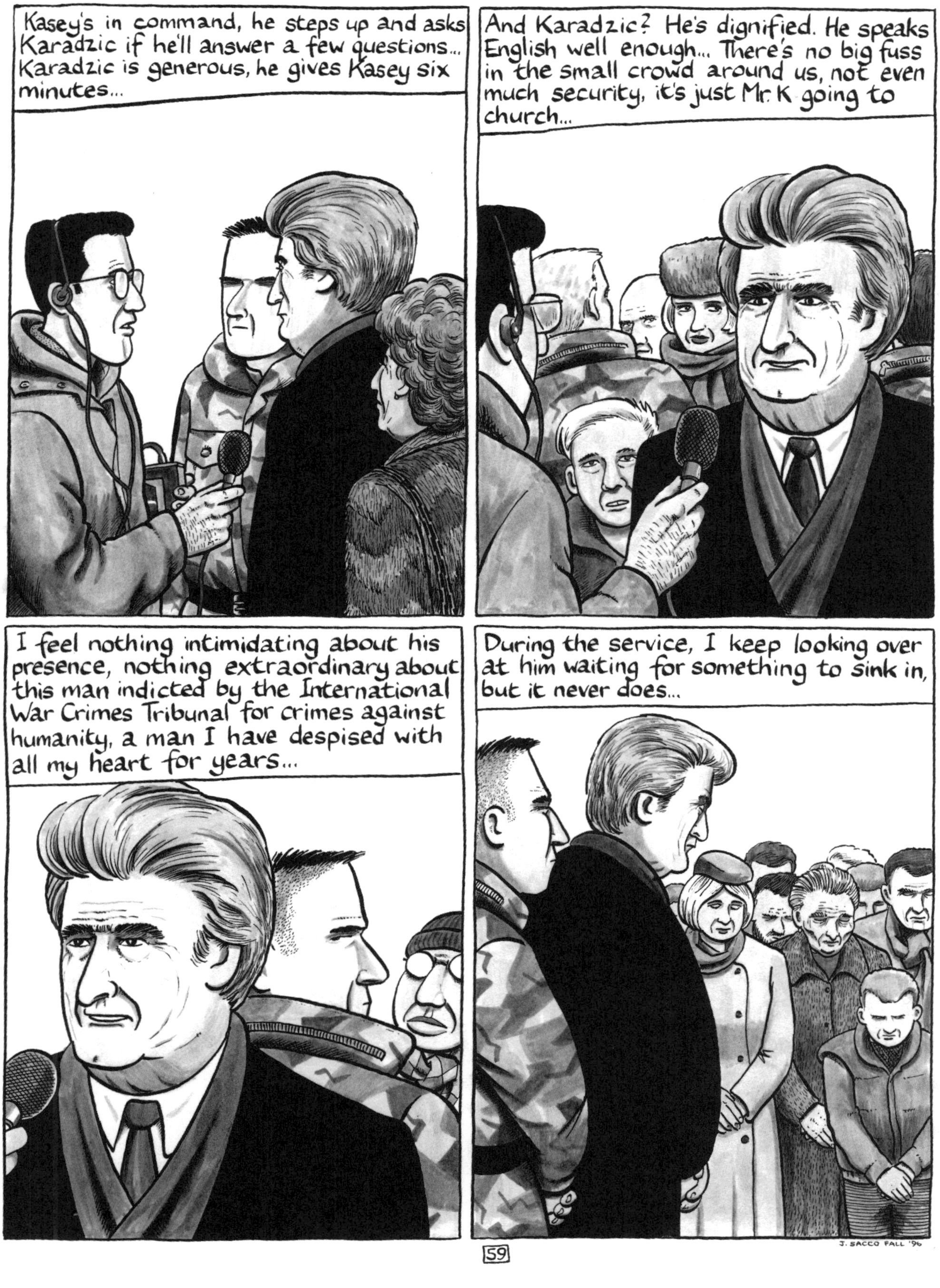
Kasey's in command, he steps up and asks Karadzic if he'll answer a few questions... Karadzic is generous, he gives Kasey six minutes...
And Karadzic? He's dignified. He speaks English well enough... There's no big fuss in the small crowd around us, not even much security, it's just Mr. K going to church...
I feel nothing intimidating about his presence, nothing extraordinary about this man indicted by the International War Crimes Tribunal for crimes against humanity, a man I have despised with all my heart for years...
During the service, I keep looking over at him waiting for something to sink in, but it never does...
J. SACCO FALL '96

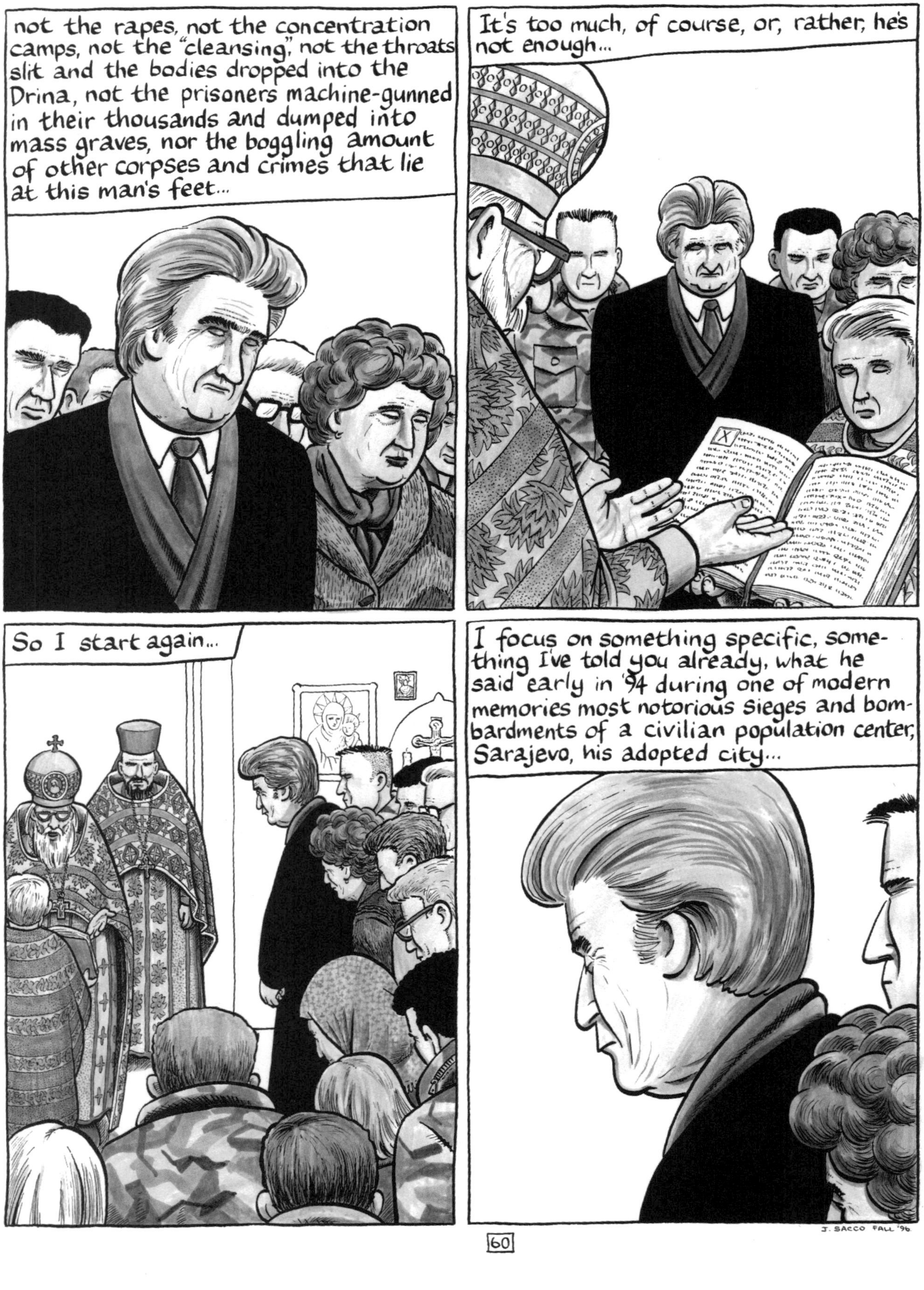
not the rapes, not the concentration camps, not the "cleansing," not the throats slit and the bodies dropped into the Drina, not the prisoners machine-gunned in their thousands and dumped into mass graves, nor the boggling amount of other corpses and crimes that lie at this man's feet...
It's too much, of course, or, rather, he's not enough...
So I start again...
I focus on something specific, something I've told you already, what he said early in '94 during one of modern memories most notorious sieges and bombardments of a civilian population center, Sarajevo, his adopted city...
J. SACCO FALL '96

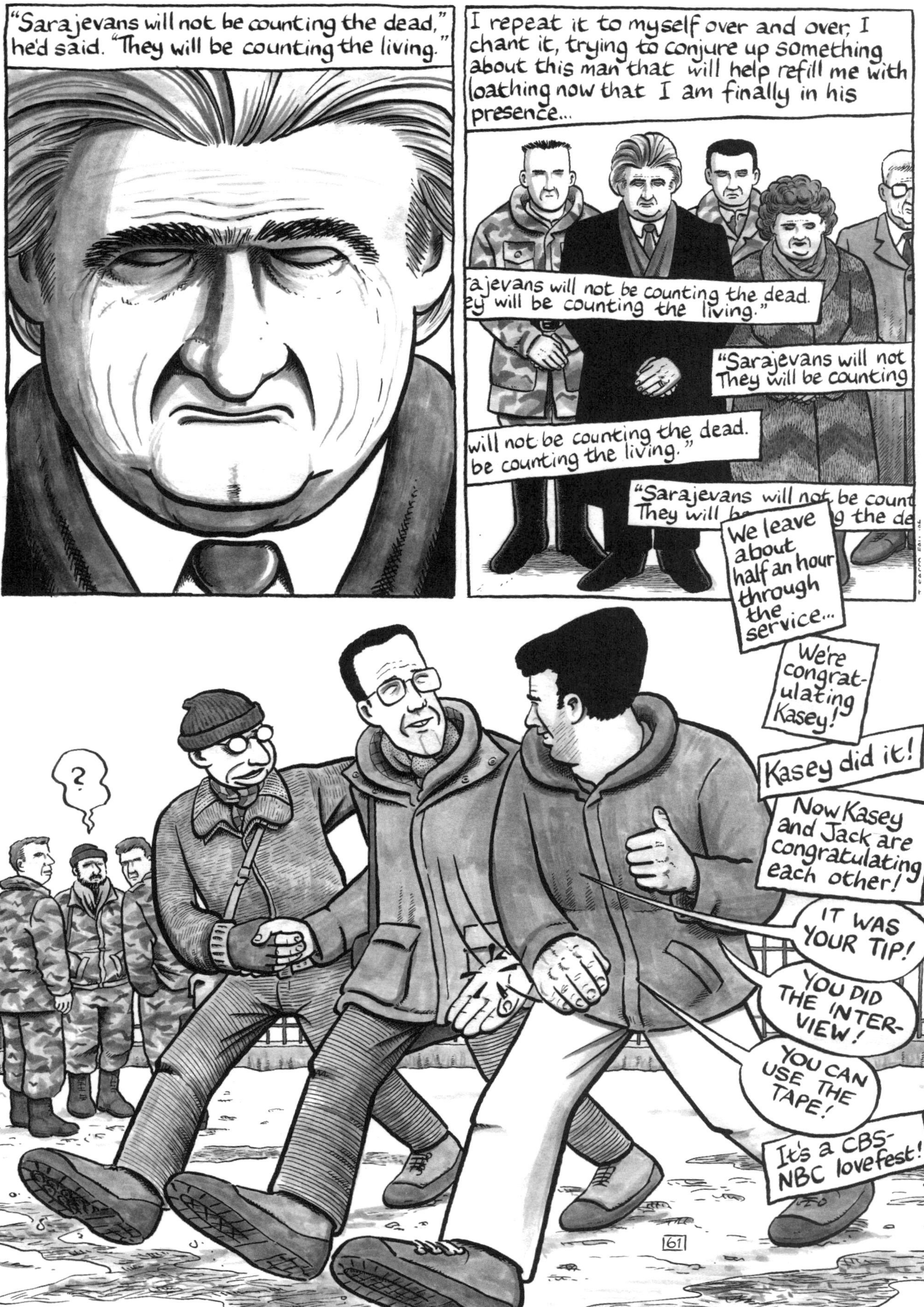
"Sarajevans will not be counting the dead," he'd said. "They will be counting the living."
I repeat it to myself over and over, I chant it, trying to conjure up something about this man that will help refill me with loathing now that I am finally in his presence...
rajevans will not be counting the dead. ey will be counting the living."
"Sarajevans will not They will be counting
will not be counting the dead. be counting the living."
"Sarajevans will not be count They will
g the de
We leave about half an hour through the service...
We're congratulating Kasey!
Kasey did it!
Now Kasey and Jack are congratulating each other!
IT WAS YOUR TIP!
YOU DID THE INTERVIEW!
YOU CAN USE THE TAPE!
It's a CBS-NBC lovefest!
?

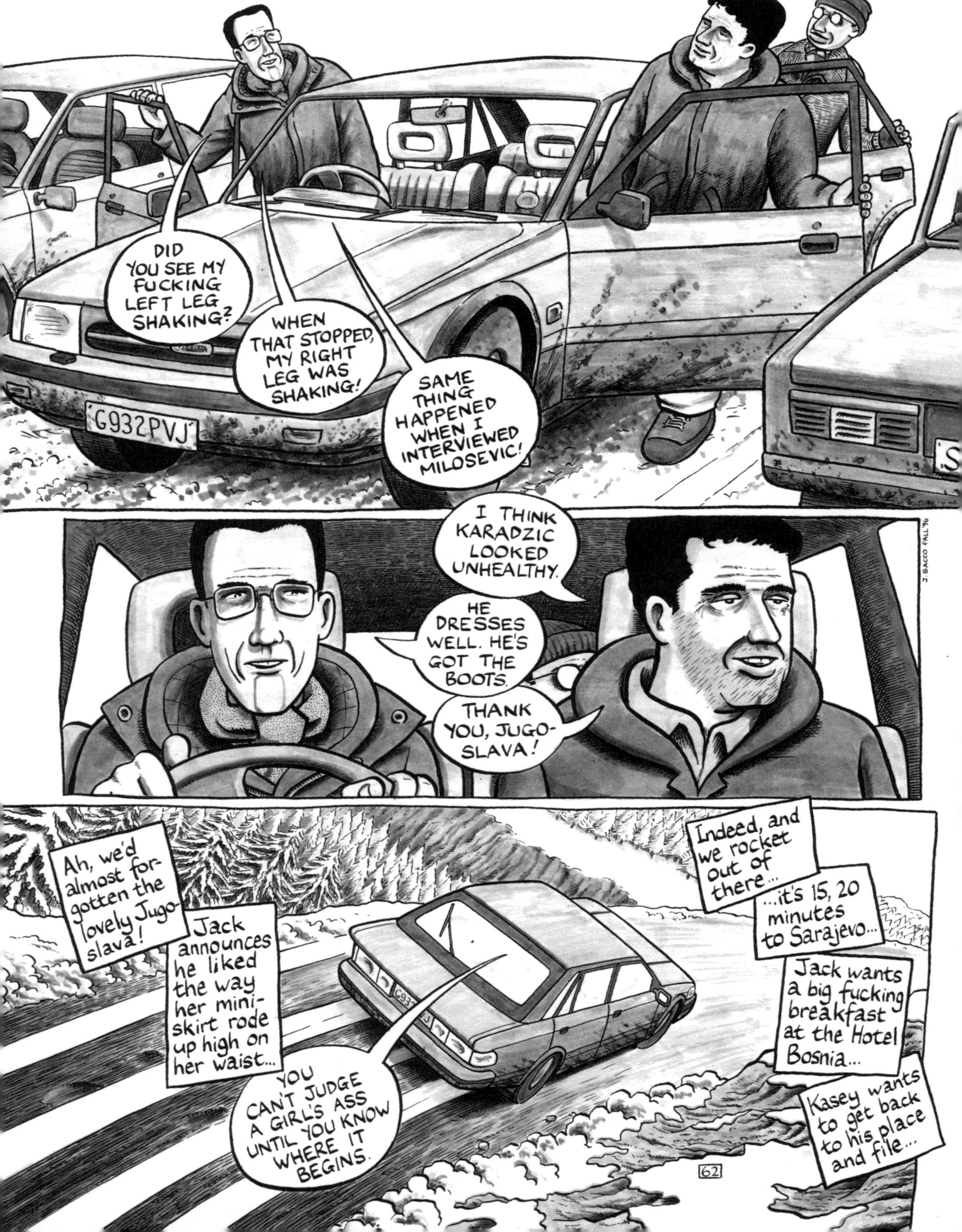
DID YOU SEE MY FUCKING LEFT LEG SHAKING?
WHEN THAT STOPPED, MY RIGHT LEG WAS SHAKING!
SAME THING HAPPENED WHEN I INTERVIEWED MILOSEVIC!
G932PVJ
I THINK KARADZIC LOOKED UNHEALTHY.
HE DRESSES WELL. HE'S GOT THE BOOTS.
THANK YOU, JUGO-SLAVA!
J. SACCO FALL '96
Ah, we'd almost forgotten the lovely Jugoslava!
Jack announces he liked the way her mini-skirt rode up high on her waist...
YOU CAN'T JUDGE A GIRL'S ASS UNTIL YOU KNOW WHERE IT BEGINS.
Indeed, and we rocket out of there...
...it's 15, 20 minutes to Sarajevo...
Jack wants a big fucking breakfast at the Hotel Bosnia...
Kasey wants to get back to his place and file...

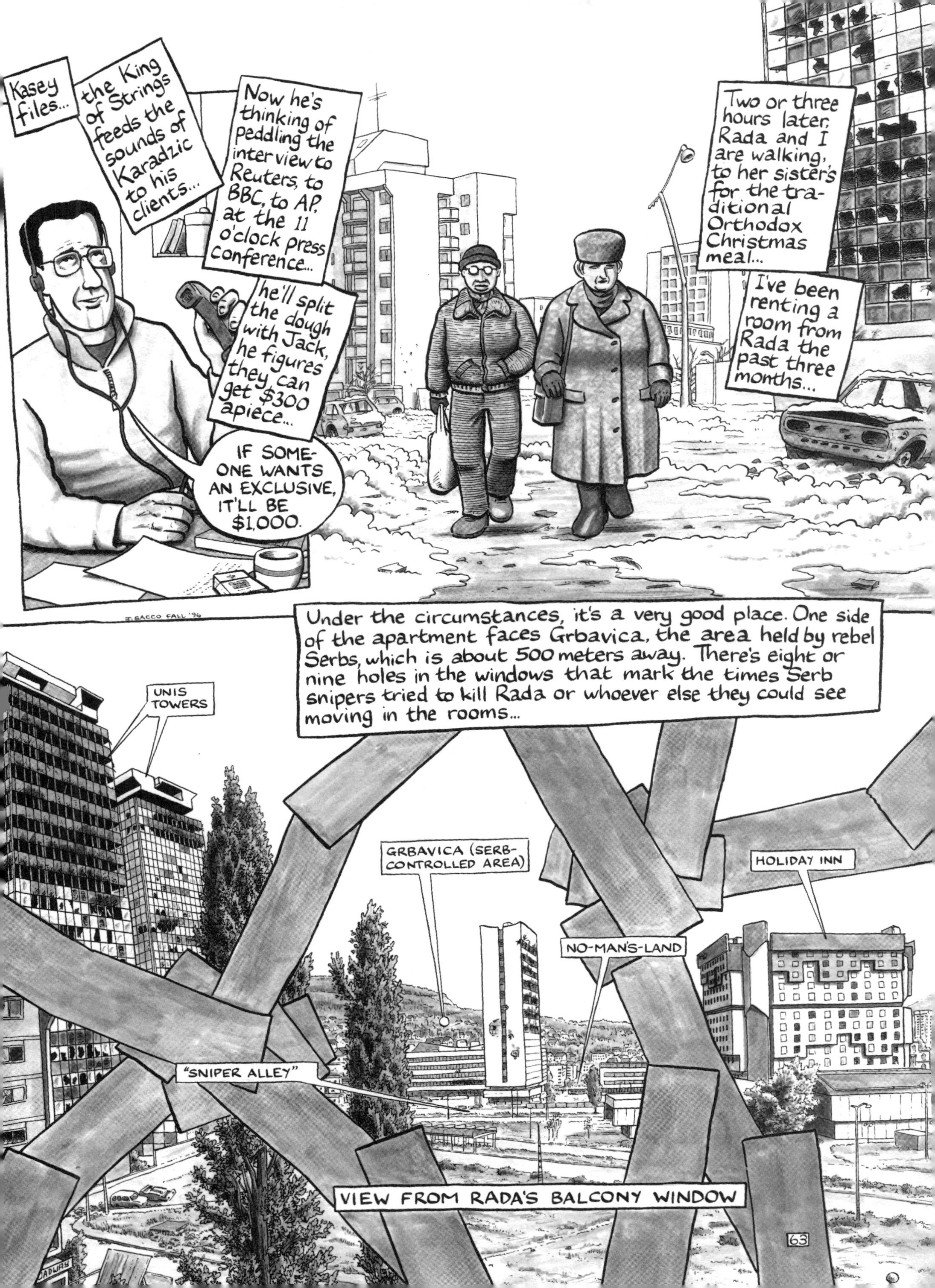

Kasey files...
the King of Strings feeds the sounds of Karadzic to his clients...
Now he's thinking of peddling the interview to Reuters, to BBC, to AP, at the 11 o'clock press conference...
he'll split the dough with Jack, he figures they can get $300 apiece...
IF SOMEONE WANTS AN EXCLUSIVE, IT'LL BE $1,000.
Two or three hours later, Rada and I are walking, to her sister's for the traditional Orthodox Christmas meal...
I've been renting a room from Rada the past three months...
J. SACCO FALL '96
Under the circumstances, it's a very good place. One side of the apartment faces Grbavica, the area held by rebel Serbs, which is about 500 meters away. There's eight or nine holes in the windows that mark the times Serb snipers tried to kill Rada or whoever else they could see moving in the rooms...
UNIS TOWERS
GRBAVICA (SERB-CONTROLLED AREA)
HOLIDAY INN
NO-MAN'S-LAND
"SNIPER ALLEY"
VIEW FROM RADA'S BALCONY WINDOW

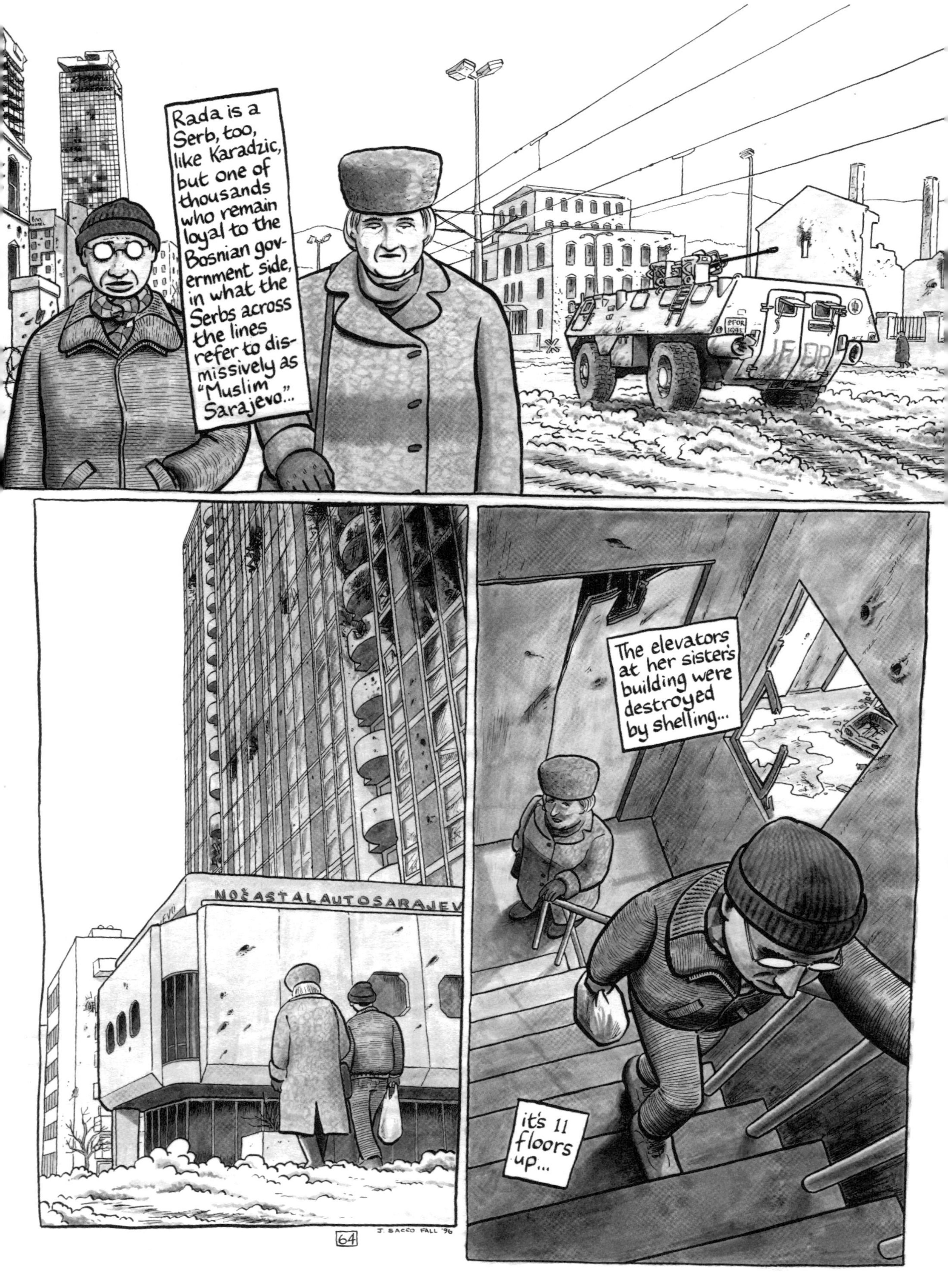
Rada is a Serb, too, like Karadzic, but one of thousands who remain loyal to the Bosnian government side, in what the Serbs across the lines refer to dismissively as "Muslim" Sarajevo...
NOŠASTALAUTOSARAJEV
The elevators at her sister's building were destroyed by shelling...
it's 11 floors up...

J. SACCO FALL '96

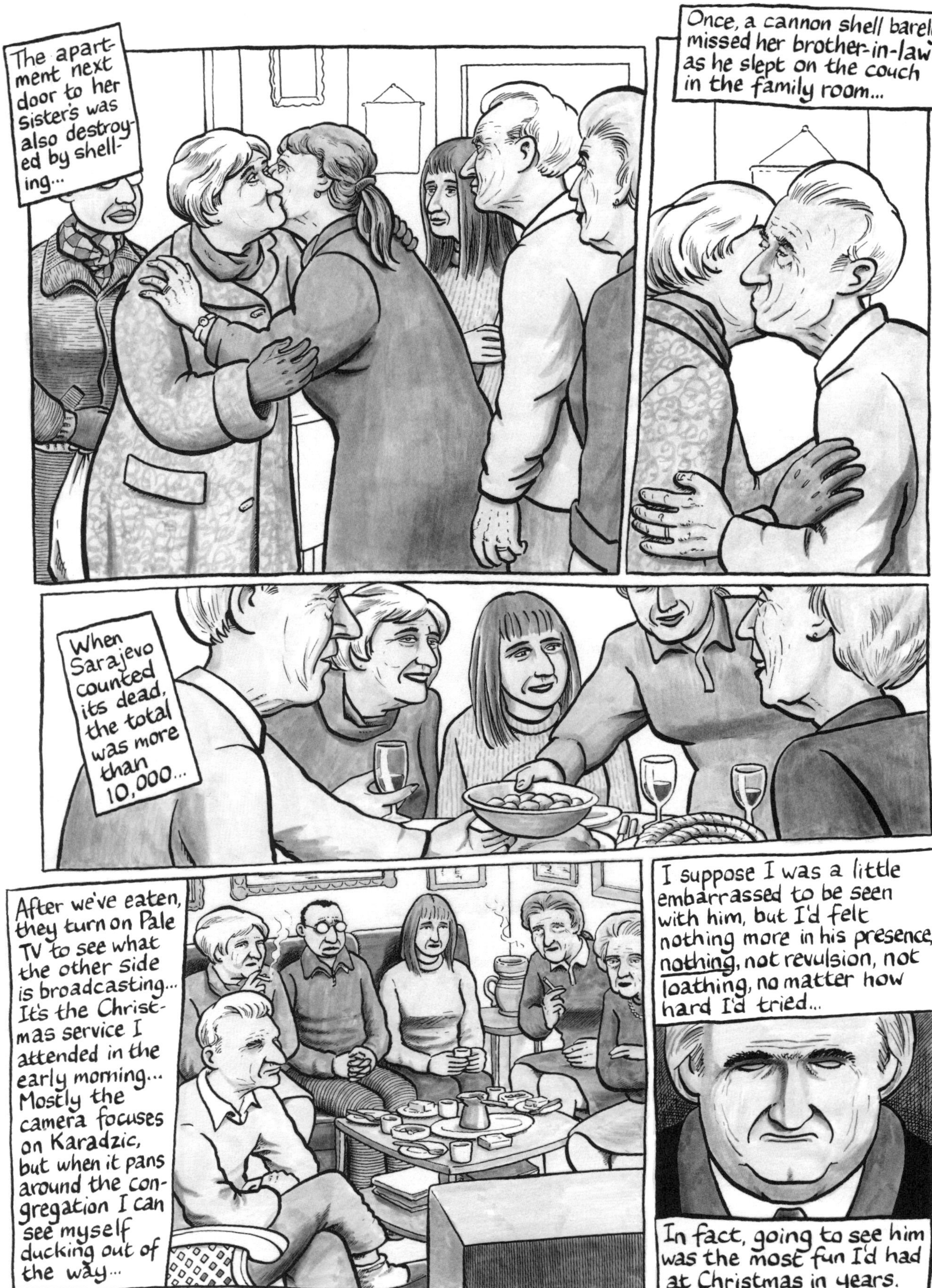

The apartment next door to her sister's was also destroyed by shelling...
Once, a cannon shell barely missed her brother-in-law as he slept on the couch in the family room...
When Sarajevo counted its dead, the total was more than 10,000...
After we've eaten, they turn on Pale TV to see what the other side is broadcasting... It's the Christmas service I attended in the early morning... Mostly the camera focuses on Karadzic, but when it pans around the congregation I can see myself ducking out of the way...
I suppose I was a little embarrassed to be seen with him, but I'd felt nothing more in his presence, nothing, not revulsion, not loathing, no matter how hard I'd tried...
In fact, going to see him was the most fun I'd had at Christmas in years.
J. SACCO FALL '96

AFTERWORD

BY THE TIME I ARRIVED IN SARAJEVO IN LATE SEPTEMBER 1995, the shelling and sniping had mostly died down though the killing elsewhere in the country persisted until a mid-October cease-fire. I remained in Bosnia until early February 1996, by which time a formal peace agreement had been signed and the uneasy post-war period had begun.

The two stories collected in this book — which I consider, more or less, profiles — were written and drawn in 1996 and 1997. 'Christmas With Karadzic' was completed first, but here I place it second because chronologically speaking its events took place after the war was officially over and later than the beginning of my friendship with Soba.

WHERE ARE THEY NOW?

The International Criminal Tribunal for the Former Yugoslavia in The Hague issued its indictments for genocide and crimes against humanity against Radovan Karadzic, head of the self-declared Bosnian Serb state, Republika Srpska, in 1995. My colleagues and I managed to track him down in January 1996. In July of that year, The Hague court issued an international arrest warrant for Karadzic, and he dropped out of sight. On a number of occasions, NATO-led peacekeepers have swooped onto his suspected hiding places, but as of this writing — nine years after he was indicted — he remains at large.

In 1999, his former benefactor, Slobodan Milosevic, the president of Serbia and then Yugoslavia, was indicted for war crimes in Kosovo. He was ousted from power following popular protests by the Serbian people and handed over to The Hague court in 2001. Indictments for genocide in Bosnia and war crimes in Croatia were added to the charges against him. He is currently on trial.

Soba has come a long way since 1995. Recently he wrote to me, "During the war, just thinking about going to the seaside was science fiction. Now, when I remember the war for just a second, I get scared, panicky. I can't imagine that I was sleeping with my Kalashnikov for three years. Life goes on, people changed. I never thought I would change." Even after the war, Soba wrote, "I never felt I would have the strength to leave Sarajevo." But Soba did travel, and eventually European galleries began to take note of his artwork, which had literally been shaped by the necessity of working with the trash and shrapnel he had found around him. Soba was invited to a residency at the Rijksacademia in Amsterdam, and he has shown his work at the Musee d'Art Moderne de la Ville de Paris and the 2003 Venice Biennal, among other prominent exhibitions. He moved to New York City with the photographer Leslie Fratkin, whom he met in Sarajevo at the end of the war. At first, "I found myself fighting for survival, working in the moving business, carrying heavy furniture up seven floors on hot summer days. In those moments I thought how the war was easier and better than this. Back in Sarajevo, everybody thinks that I'm driving a Jaguar, but the reality is totally different." Soba is no longer moving furniture, and he continues his artistic endeavours with increasing success. "Now, I'm very optimistic about my life. There are great things happening all the time. Many art pieces are being produced, many exhibitions are waiting for me, many trips are coming, exciting new friendships, and all the things one could want. This is all thanks to Leslie. She carried me through tons of shit." As for Sarajevo, Soba says, "Over there, I'm done," but, "I still love Sarajevo. I will always love it."

You can see some of Soba's earlier artwork at the Sarajevo Center for Contemporary Arts website, www.scca.ba/artistfiles/soba/ok/index.htm

DEDICATIONS

When the 'Soba' comic was first published in 1998, I dedicated it to Soba, of course, and also to the Zaimovic family in Sarajevo, who, as I wrote then, "reminded me in their quiet way that culture and dignity still exist in Europe, and who welcomed me into their warm home at a time of great personal loss." That dedication remains.

'Christmas With Karadzic' was published in 1997 without a dedication. But now I would like to dedicate that story to the people at the International Criminal Tribunal for the Former Yugoslavia and all those who are working to arrest Radovan Karadzic.

Joe Sacco
November 2004

ABOUT THE AUTHOR

JOE SACCO WAS BORN IN MALTA IN 1960. He studied at the University of Oregon and graduated with a degree in journalism. Sacco traveled extensively in the 1980s, living in Europe where he worked as a cartoonist, an editor, and poster artist.

After traveling to the Middle East in the early 1990s, Sacco came away from Israel and the occupied territories with the material that would make up his groundbreaking graphic novel PALESTINE (1995, Fantagraphics), for which he received the American Book Award in 1996.

In 1995, Sacco traveled to Sarajevo and its surrounding areas. There he began his book SAFE AREA GORAZDE (2000, Fantagraphics), which details the tragic siege of one of the "Safe Areas" by Bosnian Serb forces. In 2001, Sacco was awarded a grant by the John Simon Guggenheim Memorial Foundation that allowed him to return to Bosnia for additional research for his graphic novel THE FIXER (2003, Drawn & Quarterly). In THE FIXER, Sacco profiled Neven, a one-time soldier for a local warlord who took Western journalists to the front lines of the conflict.

Sacco resides in Portland, Oregon and recently completed a story on Chechen refugees based on a trip he took to Ingushetia, a republic that borders Chechnya. The story will be for I LIVE HERE, an upcoming book that will benefit Amnesty International. Currently, he is at work on a book on Rafah, a town and refugee camp in the Gaza Strip.

Sacco's work has been exhibited in art galleries and universities around the world, and he has lectured on political conflict, journalism, and the art of comics.

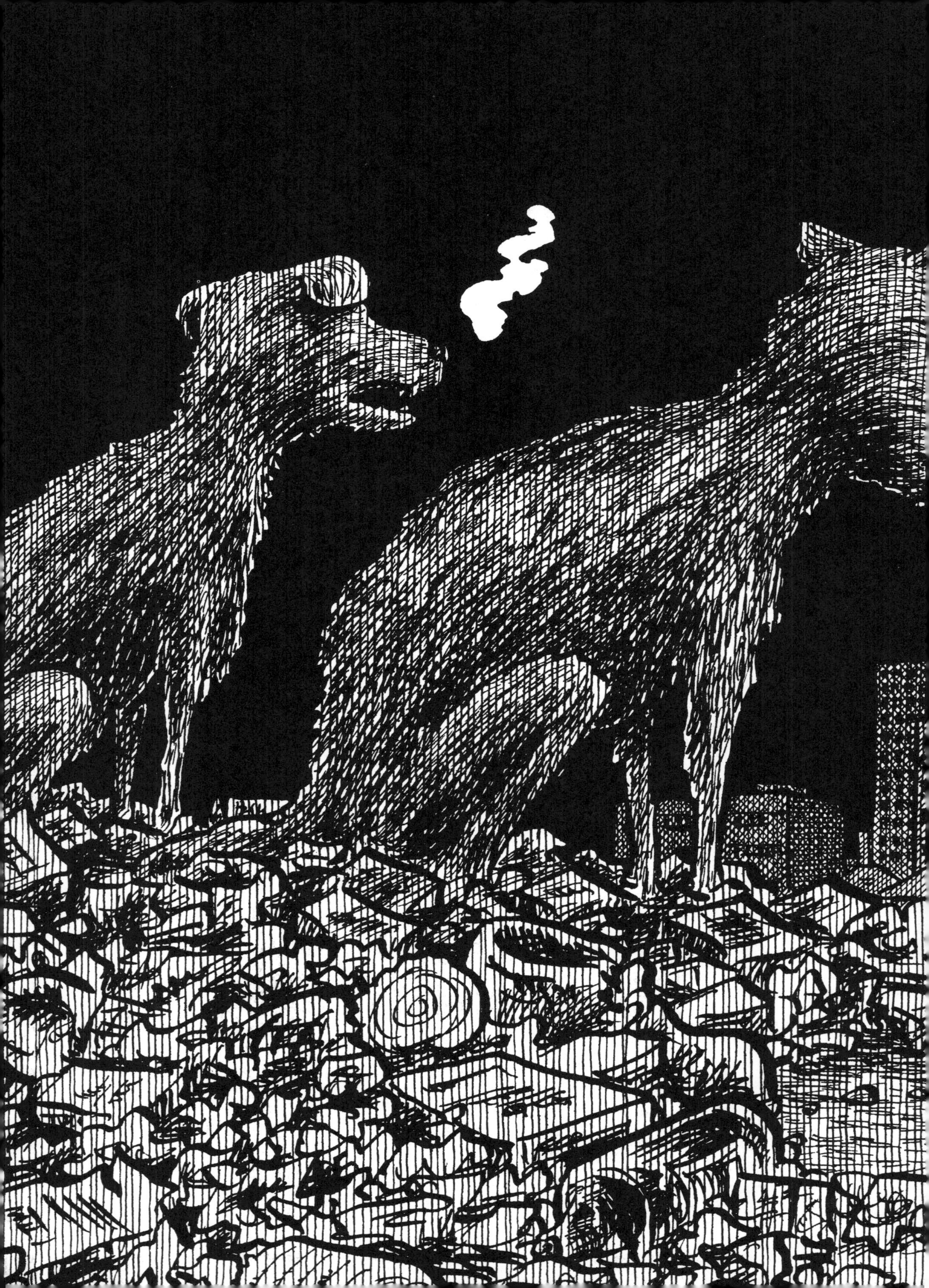